REGENTS CRIT

General Editor: J

CRITICAL WRITINGS OF
FORD MADOX FORD

Critical Writings of
Ford Madox Ford

Edited by

FRANK MACSHANE

UNIVERSITY OF NEBRASKA PRESS · LINCOLN

Thanks are due Miss Janice Biala for permission to reprint the following previously published items from the writings of Ford Madox Ford: Selected passages from *The English Novel* (Philadelphia: J. B. Lippincott Co., 1929); "The Reader" in *The Transatlantic Review* (October 1924); "On Impressionism" in *Poetry and Drama* (June, December 1914); "Techniques" in *The Southern Review* (July 1935); selected passages from *Joseph Conrad: A Personal Remembrance* (London: Duckworth and Co., 1924); a letter to John Galsworthy quoted in H. V. Marrot, *The Life and Letters of John Galsworthy* (London: Heinemann Ltd., 1935); selections from letters to Sir Herbert Read, originally published in Herbert Read, *Annals of Innocence and Experience* (London: Faber and Faber, Ltd., 1940); "Henry James" in *Portraits from Life* (Boston: Houghton Mifflin Co., 1937), copyright 1936, 1937 by Houghton Mifflin Co.; "Introduction" to Ernest Hemingway, *A Farewell to Arms* (New York: Random House, Inc., 1932), copyright 1932 by Random House, Inc.; "Impressionism—Some Speculations" in *Poetry* (August, September 1913); and selected passages from *The March of Literature* (London: George Allen and Unwin, Ltd., 1939, 1947).

Publishers on the Plains

UNP

MANUFACTURED IN THE UNITED STATES OF AMERICA

Regents Critics Series

The Regents Critics Series provides reading texts of significant literary critics in the Western tradition. The series treats criticism as a useful tool: an introduction to the critic's own poetry and prose if he is a poet or novelist, an introduction to other work in his day if he is more judge than creator. Nowhere is criticism regarded as an end in it self but as what it is—a means to the understanding of the language of art as it has existed and been understood in various periods and societies.

Each volume includes a scholarly introduction which describes how the work collected came to be written, and suggests its uses. All texts are edited in the most conservative fashion consonant with the production of a good reading text; and all translated texts observe the dictum that the letter gives life and the spirit kills when a technical or rigorous passage is being put into English. Other types of passages may be more freely treated. Footnoting and other scholarly paraphernalia are restricted to the essential minimum. Such features as a bibliographical checklist or an index are carried where they are appropriate to the work in hand. If a volume is the first collection of the author's critical writing, this is noted in the bibliographical data.

PAUL A. OLSON

University of Nebraska

Contents

Introduction

There is a certain poetic justice in the fact that this collection of an English novelist's critical writings is appearing for the first time in the State of Nebraska, for from about 1923 until his death in 1939, Ford Madox Ford continuously asserted that the best writing in English of those years was being produced not by the inhabitants of the older literary centres like London, New York, and Boston, but by men and women who were born west of the Hudson River. The names of Ernest Hemingway, Carl Sandburg, John Dos Passos, James Farrell, Glenway Wescott, Theodore Dreiser, Ring Lardner, Sherwood Anderson, Sinclair Lewis, and Scott Fitzgerald, all of whom came from the Middle West, suggest that Ford was not far wrong in his literary judgment.

Early in his career Ford had become acquainted with two American writers, Stephen Crane and Henry James, both of whom were then living in England, and during the course of his first trip to the United States in 1906, he met Nebraska's Willa Cather, who at the time was working for *McClure's Magazine* in New York. After his return to England and his assumption of the editorship of *The English Review,* he encountered a number of other Mid-Western writers, among them Ezra Pound of Idaho, T. S. Eliot of Missouri, and John Gould Fletcher of Arkansas. It was not until 1924, however, when he became editor of *The Transatlantic Review* in Paris, that he became convinced of the dominance over Anglo-Saxon literature of writing emanating from the Middle West and South. Through his friendship with American writers like Katherine Anne Porter, Caroline Gordon, and Allen Tate, at the end of his life he even took a position as artist-in-residence at a small college in Michigan.

But lest this emphasis seem chauvinistic—and therefore not in keeping with Ford's own belief in an international republic of letters—it would be well to consider his standards as a literary critic. Born into an artistic circle dominated by views originally disseminated by the Pre-Raphaelite Brotherhood, Ford from the very beginning was anti-academic. He inherited a distaste for academic painting from his grandfather, Ford Madox Brown, and as a youth in Germany, he observed with horror the way in which German professors substituted philology for literary appreciation. He thus naturally adopted an attitude of protest against the propagation of accepted ideas and the use of conventional forms. Furthermore, as a poet and novelist, he belonged to a group of writers who were entirely out of sympathy with the academic establishment of London which in the early years of the century was represented by the literary journals and quarterlies. His critical views, in short, were those he developed as a practicing artist and as a young man passionately addicted to uninhibited and therefore professional literary discussion.

The standards he applied—at least to fiction—were those he had himself adopted after reading Continental novelists of the nineteenth century, notably Stendhal, Turgenev, Flaubert, and Maupassant. His exposure to these writers and his endless discussions with his collaborator, Joseph Conrad, led him to believe that the function of writing was simply to give an objective presentation of actuality; there was to be no attempt on the part of the author to use his work as a vehicle for moralizing or instruction. His assumption of this attitude was in part a reaction against English fiction since the eighteenth century. Explicitly or implicitly, most novelists of this period, including Fielding, Dickens, and Thackeray, were didactic. They constructed their novels so as to defend the moral values of Protestant Christianity and the English social codes which accompanied them. Consciously moralistic, they manipulated their plots so that "goodness" and "virtue" would always triumph in the end.

Having been exposed to Continental fiction, Ford believed that such English novels were generally falsifications of reality. England had not experienced a social revolution similar to that of the French in 1789; nor had it known the results of violently contradictory social systems such as had appeared in France before and after Napoleon. Nevertheless, in fact if not in fiction,

England had slowly emerged into the modern age. Most English novelists, however, had failed to take stock of changed conditions and continued to write in terms of a system of social values that was out of date. Whereas French novelists like Stendhal and Flaubert had been forced to deal with situations in which they found no absolute truths, and had therefore attempted to provide a picture of life containing a multiplicity of values, each containing a certain amount of truth, most English novelists continued to represent the values of the eighteenth century. The English novel remained relatively static while its French counterpart developed. It became a vehicle for the expression of divergent ideas and the actual arena in which the reader could evaluate contradictory attitudes. The French novel emphasized pluralism and complication: it did not present life as a simple opposition of good and evil.

Anxious to develop the English novel along the lines already laid out by the French and to a certain extent by Henry James, Ford constantly reiterated his belief that the job of the novelist was simply to present life as the shimmering affair it actually was —without absolute truths and without heroes and villains. In accomplishing this end, accuracy was of paramount importance: hence Ford's never-ending search for a new form for the novel and his concentration upon what he called "rendering" as against description, since rendering was an attempt to be objective. Ford's concern for technique embraced virtually every aspect of imaginative writing, from the necessity of capturing the rhythm and psychology of ordinary conversation to the need for social, political and moral "justification" of characters. Yet in his desire to present a sense of twentieth-century actuality, Ford did not subscribe to the methods of Emile Zola; nor, indeed, to those of George Gissing and George Moore. His literary instincts and his psychological insights made him prefer an artistically pleasing *impression* of reality to a thoroughly documented transcript of it. In short, what Ford believed the novelist had to do was to approach his own work in the same manner as a sculptor or painter approaches his: the subject matter is not important; what counts is in the way in which it is presented. "I am interested only in how to write," he once said, "and . . . I care nothing—but nothing in the world!—what a man writes about."

Given this attitude, Ford naturally believed that the proper—and only—function of the critic was to discuss the methods, or techniques, employed in a work of art. He expressed this view in a letter to his friend, Edward Garnett, who at the turn of the century was a publisher's reader and the editor of a series of monographs on painting:

The idea keeps booming in my head: Why shouldn't there be a popular Library of Literature on the lines of yr. Library of Art?—conceived on the broad general idea of making manifest, to the most unintelligent, how great writers *get their effects.* As distinct from the general line of tub-thumping about moral purposes, the number of feet in a verse, or the amiable and noble ideas entertained, by said Great Writers, of Elevating and making the world a better place.

The idea, I say, keeps booming in my head—why couldn't one make some sort of nucleus, just some little attempt at forming a small heap on which people could stand and get a point of view with their heads a few inches above the moral atmosphere of these Islands.

It was to be some years before Ford himself would be able to form such a nucleus in *The English Review,* but this early concern illustrates the way in which he anticipated the New Critics of a later generation. Yet Ford was not, of course, a critic like John Crowe Ransom or Dr. Leavis: as an enthusiastic pioneer, he was incapable of the balanced and scholarly assessment that characterizes their criticism. A writer himself, he believed that the critic should also be a mentor: he should actually help other authors to improve their work. Moreover, he was temperamentally ill-suited to inditing calmly considered essays on a man's work; he could not suppress personal anecdote or fictitious illustrative material. Robie Macaulay, who was one of Ford's students in 1938, characterized his critical approach in this way:

Ford's method of teaching was narrative and anecdotal. Almost any question could be answered or any idea presented in the form of a story and he was ill at ease in any more abstract conversation. . . . Usually his stories were not simple illustrations of the point: they contained a great many relative and tangential things. Thus, a student asking a question about drama, might get as an answer a quite involved and probably half-imaginary story about Goethe that seemed to end up a considerable distance from the original question. If he thought about it, however, he would realise that along the way Ford had introduced a dozen relevant ideas and, although he had never given a direct answer, he had given an extraordinarily complete one.

In short, Ford was not a critic in the first instance. Rather he was a poet and a novelist whose critical writings were a by-product of his imaginative work. As a result, the value of his criticism has sometimes been questioned. Rebecca West, for example, observed:

I don't think Ford was a great critic, I don't think it was in his power to be so because of his transforming memory which altered everything. A man can hardly say anything valuable about the great works of literature if he cannot remember a single one of them as they were written. I had the fresh memory of youth when I talked with Ford, and I hardly remember a single occasion when he discussed a great book without it presently emerging that he had a totally false impression of its theme or that he had added or subtracted from the author's list of characters.

On the other hand, Sir Compton Mackenzie wrote: "When I consider the critical minds with which I have come into contact I find that I have no hesitation in declaring that of the many judgments I have listened to on literature, the least fallible of all were Ford Madox Ford's."

Seemingly contradictory, these two statements are really complementary. For Ford believed that one of the principal functions of criticism was to awaken the critical faculties of others. He was always anxious to establish "movements" in which artistic problems could be publicly aired, and he talked endlessly with his friends about technique. The results were slow in coming, but in the end, Ford's influence was considerable: it appears in the literary polemics of Ezra Pound, and it appears in the work of the Imagist poets. It may also be found, directly or indirectly, in the work of numerous novelists younger than himself—in Hemingway and Caroline Gordon; in Faulkner and Joyce.

Yet as a critic, Ford was too much the experimental writer to dogmatize. In his preface to *The English Novel,* he warned students of literature not to accept his judgments as incontestably true. Instead, he hoped that his statements would so excite the reader that he would himself start to think seriously about them and thus establish his own critical attitude. Profoundly distrustful of accepted ideas, Ford did all in his power to dislodge them, and most of his critical and social writings were designed with this end in view. As an imaginative artist, Ford was always excited by literature—he frequently observed of himself that he was "an old man mad about writing." He looked upon all good literature as contemporary, and considered great writers not as dead figures from the past appearing in histories of literature, but as living men who had things to say to modern men even though they had died physically five hundred years before. The thrill of discovery and the delight with which Ford regarded literary masterpieces did not lend themselves to calm assessment. The passionate enthusiasm with which he approached his subject always shone through. Thus, although Ford's critical writing may seem exaggerated and wrong-headed in some respects, it is never dull. Nowhere is his attitude better expressed than in the statement with which he opened his critical study of Henry James. "Mr. James," he said, "is the greatest of living writers and in consequence, for me, the greatest of living men." What better proof that literature mattered?

A Note on the Text

The texts of the Ford selections are presented here as in their original manuscript or printed form except for the correction of a few obvious misspellings and typographical errors. A bibliographical note follows each selection.

FRANK MACSHANE

University of California, Berkeley

THE TRADITIONS OF THE NOVEL

In the following selections, three asterisks (* * *) indicate that a portion of the original has been omitted.

The English Novel

During his lifetime, Ford wrote a number of general assessments of literature, of which The English Novel *(1929) proved to be the most popular and successful. Based on a series of lectures given in the United States following the publication of his best-selling Tietjens novels, it was at one time widely used as supplementary reading in university courses dealing with the novel. Ford himself was amused by this development, and in the English edition of 1930, he observed in his prefatory remarks that "The young, earnest student of literature for professional purposes should, if he desires good marks, write in his thesis for examination pretty well the opposite of what I have here set down." Though still not without its relevance in some places, this warning need not be taken so seriously today, for the view of the novel here presented has become acceptable in most academic circles. That it has become acceptable may be attributed in part to Ford's own pioneering efforts as a critic which in turn helped plant the seeds of the New Criticism.*

In the selections here reprinted, Ford examines both the central English tradition in the novel and its counterpart on the Continent, especially in France, and draws conclusions which constitute his own artistic standards.

* * * For Richardson I have the profoundest respect that amounts as nearly as possible to an affection—if that is to say it is possible to have an affection for a man whose death preceded one's birth by one hundred and twelve years. I do not apologize for the fact that *Pamela* is my personal favourite whereas the graver critics and mankind in general prefer *Clarissa*. By that the reader need not be guided but he should certainly pay a good deal of attention to the works of Richardson—and indeed to Richardson himself.

That tranquil person came into the world in 1689—twenty-seven or eight years after the birth of Defoe and one year after the death of Bunyan. But whereas both of his predecessors seem to strike notes almost entirely of the seventeenth century Richardson seems to be absolutely of the eighteenth and, with him sentimentality was born in the world of the novel. That perhaps was necessary to an age that banished if not conventional, then at least doctrinal, moralizings to its collections of sermons in volume form. For them of course there was a prodigious demand.

Of course, too, it would be wrong to assert that moralizing found no place in the novels of Richardson since the high moral purpose breathes from every pore of his pages. But it was not with moralizing that he made his primary appeal as had been the case with Bunyan, nor was it likely that had he so done he would have found many readers. No, it is his sentimentalizing that is his E string.

Against that I have nothing to say. Anglo-Saxons are sentimentalists before everything and in all their arts, and it is probable that without sentimentality as an ingredient no Anglo-Saxon artist could work: certainly he could have no appeal. To produce national masterpieces in paint Turner must bathe his canvasses deep in that gentle fluid; the English lyric is a marvel of sentimentality and so is English domestic architecture with its mellow—or mellowed!—red brick, its dovecotes, its south walls for netted fruits. So the first of modern novelists must be one of the greatest of sentimentalists. And on those lines his appeal is universal and everlasting.

Only today an American left the ship on which I am writing in the port of Lisbon and, I happening to mention because he was in my mind the name of Richardson, this American—professor at that and practitioner of a sister art—this American gentleman assured me solemnly that he read *Clarissa Harlowe* at least twice every year and cried often during each reading. Now there must be some reason for this phenomenon which appears very singular. It is not, however, rare, for the hottest literary discussions I have ever had in England—where of course the discussion of literature is not in good form—have been with laymen like professors or lawyers as to the relative merits of *Pamela* and *Clarissa*.

For me, I read Richardson for a hearty and wholesome dose of sentimentality and if one does that one may as well have that quality laid on as thickly as it will go. And it seems to me that the history of a serving maid who resists her master's efforts at seduction and ultimately forces him to marry her is a more senti-mental affair than that of a young lady of quality who permits herself to be seduced by a relatively commonplace Lothario. For myself I have always felt inclined to cheer over the success of the one young female rather than to weep for the tribulations of the other. Pamela certainly seems to be the more sporting character of the two.

Still, one should perhaps not read Richardson for his sporting quality and that sort of thing is really no affair of mine. The main point is that Samuel Richardson is still read and read with enthusiasm. I have even met persons who were engrossed by the conversations in the Cedar Parlour of *Sir Charles Grandison*.

That Richardson's tender muse was at times too much for the robuster and more cynical taste of his age is proved by the fact that Fielding's first famous novel was begun as a parody on the first famous novel of Richardson. By that date the novel of com-merce was well on the way to the market and young ladies lying on sofas reading the latest fiction or furiously sending their maids to the circulating libraries for the next five volumes of their latest favourite—such young ladies were familiar features of the social landscape. Literature had in fact become a sound, if not an im-mensely lucrative, proposition.

And it is pleasant to think that, happy as he was in every-thing that he touched, Richardson was not only novelist but printer and publisher and quite a warm business man in either capacity. He was too a favourite correspondent and companion of innumerable young ladies who consulted him as to their ama-tory predicaments and because of that he is not only the first novelist in the modern sense of the word but also the first literary feminist. You might call him an eighteenth century Henry James and not go so far wrong.

At any rate, he stands alone as a modern novelist and had in England neither appreciable imitators nor rivals until the arrival on the scene of the author of the Barchester Towers series.

Except for Smollett—whom it is hopeless to expect Anglo-Saxon readers to appreciate or to consume, the main stream of development of the novel passed once more to the Continent of Europe. Smollett begat Captain Marryat who was one of the greatest of English novelists and is therefore regarded as a writer for boys, Smollett himself being most prized by the purveyors of books called 'curious' in second-hand catalogues.

Before, however, considering Diderot, Stendhal, Chauteaubriand, and Flaubert, all avowed followers of the Author of *Clarissa* it might be as well to think a little about Fielding—as at once a dreadful example of how not to do things and as the begetter of Thackeray and the product that it is convenient to call the nuvvle as opposed to the novel. For at about the date of the births of Napoleon, Wellington, Ney, and many others who began the modern world, and just a little after the death of Richardson, and just a little before the birth of the North American Republic, and still a little more before the Cæsarian operation that produced the French Republic, distinct cleavages began to make themselves observed in the fields of writing, these eventually hardening themselves into the three main streams of the Literature of Escape from the everyday world; into the commercial product that Mamma selected for your reading, that it is convenient to call the nuvvle and that formed the immense bulk of the reading matter and finally into the modern novel which does not avoid the problems of the day and is written with some literary skill. This last Richardson begat.

And it is convenient to say that Defoe, in spite of his moralizations, was the first writer of the Literature of Escape just as Smollett and Marryat may be described as carrying it on and the young H. G. Wells and the young Rudyard Kipling as bringing it—at any rate, temporarily—to a triumphant close.

Were it not that they were avowed moralizers of a middle-to-lower-middle class type, the Fielding-to-Thackeray lineage of writers might also be regarded as purveyors of the Literature of Escape but their continually brought in passages of moralizations are such a nuisance that they cannot be ignored. Though they were both amateurs in the sense that neither knew how to write or cared anything about it, Thackeray at times projected his scenes so wonderfully that now and then he trembles dreadfully excitingly on the point of passing from the stage of purveyor of the nuvvle to that of the real novelist. And it is to be said for Fielding that although *Tom Jones* contains an immense amount of rather nauseous special-pleading the author does pack most of it away into solid wads of hypocrisy at the headings of Parts or Chapters. These can in consequence be skipped and the picaresque story with its mildly salacious details can without difficulty be followed. One might indeed almost say that Fielding was a natural story-teller whereas Thackeray was none at all. Fielding at least, like a story-teller in a school dormitory, does manage to lose himself in details of people running into and out of each others' bedrooms in hotel corridors at night—something like that. But Thackeray never could: the dread spectre of the Athenæum Club was forever in his background.

And I imagine that the greatest literary crime ever committed was Thackeray's sudden, apologetic incursion of himself into his matchless account of the manœuvres of Becky Sharp on Waterloo day in Brussels. The greatest crime that anyone perhaps ever committed! For the motive of most crimes is so obscure, so pathological or so fatalized by hereditary weakness that there is almost nothing that can not be pardoned once one has dived beneath the calm surface of things. But Thackeray as child-murderer can never be forgiven: the deeper you delve into the hidden springs of his offence the more unforgivable does he appear.

I had better perhaps explain the cause of all this emotion for the benefit of the lay reader who has not yet got at what I am writing about.

The struggle—the aspiration—of the novelist down the ages has been to evolve a water-tight convention for the frame-work of the novel. He aspires—and for centuries has aspired—so to construct his stories and so to manage their surfaces that the carried away and rapt reader shall really think himself to be in Brussels on the first of Waterloo days or in Grand Central Station waiting for the Knickerbocker Express to come in from Boston though actually he may be sitting in a cane lounge on a beach of Bermuda in December. This is not easy.

Of the three major novelists that we have hitherto examined each in his own way had a try, consciously or unconsciously, at performing this conjuring trick. Bunyan tried to do it—and succeeded remarkably well—by the simplest of story-teller's devices. He just told on in simple language using such homely images that the reader, astonished and charmed to find the circumstances of his own life typified in words and glorified by print, is seized by the homely narrative and carried clean out of himself into the world of that singular and glorious tinker.

Defoe on the other hand, in the conscious or unconscious effort to achieve a convention for the novel, adopted the biographical or autobiographical form, relying on the verisimilitude of the details that he invented to confirm the reader in the belief that his characters had really existed and so to awaken the sympathy that makes books readable. And had he possessed a little more power of projection or a little more subtlety in presenting his figures and had his writing been a little less pedestrian his works might have gained and held the power to arouse a great deal more enthusiasm than they actually do.

Richardson, going a good deal further, has left it on record that he was actually bothered by the problem of the novelistic convention and that he racked his brain a long time before arriving at the one he finally adopted. He asked himself, that is to say, how the reader was to be convinced that the author—and by analogy still more his characters—how could they know all the details that go to making up a book? If, to reduce the matter to its most elementary form, Sir Charles Grandison is walking in the Yew Walk how can he know what characters are present in and what conversations are being carried on in the Cedar Parlour and since, to satisfy the reader the author is to be supposed to be cognisant of all that passes in his novel how is *he* to know simultaneously what is happening in both places?

That at least is what bothered Richardson and what has bothered all other novelists since his day, though until quite lately no English novelist made any serious attempt to attack the problem. The method that Richardson with characteristically homespun commonsense eventually worked out was simply to cast the whole novel into correspondence, the characters exchanging letters as to events and as to their psychologies with other characters or with anyone to whom a letter could be handily addressed. In that way any character who was needed to know anything could be given the information and the author had only to let it be supposed that he had an unusual knack of getting hold of the correspondence of other people to convince the reader for all eighteenth century purposes. For in the seventeenth and eighteenth centuries, as everyone knows, everyone from Madame de Sevigné upwards and downwards addressed to everyone else letters of prodigious length and in the most excruciating detail—and Richardson himself, as we have seen, had a prodigious knowledge of the prodigious letters that eighteenth century young ladies could address to even unknown correspondents once their hearts and feelings were touched. So that although today the letter is one of the worst of methods that exist for telling a story if the dictates of probability are to be considered, Richardson may be considered to have done very well indeed with his peculiar form.

To its disadvantages in other hands we shall come in due time, but, meanwhile enormous applause is due to the author of *Pamela* for having given the matter any thought at all. And in any case his is a figure so sympathetic and so craftsmanlike that we do well to love him. He is sound, quiet, without fuss, going about his work as a carpenter goes about making a chair and in the end turning out an article of supreme symmetry and consistence. I know of no other figure in English literature—if it be not that of Trollope—who so suggests the two supreme artists of the world—Holbein and Bach.

It would be hyperbole to suggest that Richardson is as great in his art as either of the other two. He had neither their power over their materials nor their sense of the beauty of natural things. Our gratitude to him nevertheless should be great for he worked with the simplest materials and manœuvred only the most normal

of characters in the most commonplace of events and yet contrived to engross the minds of a large section of mankind. How
to do that is the problem that, Richardson having been dead a
century and a half, still engrosses the novelist.

And what more than anything is impressive about his figure
is that one knows almost nothing about it: he is as little over-
drawn as are his characters whereas the besetting sin of almost
all other English novelists from Fielding to George Meredith is
that they seem to cut their characters out with hatchets and to
colour them with the brushes of house-painters and, never, even
at that, being able to let them alone, they are perpetually pushing
their own faces and winking at you over the shoulders of Young
Blifil, Uncle Toby, the Widow Wadman, Dick Swiveller, the
Marchioness, Becky Sharp, Evan Harrington, and the rest. That
is usually applauded by orthodox Anglo-Saxon criticism and to
talk of the gallery of portraits left by this or that novelist is considered to be high praise indeed. But, as a matter of fact, the
overdrawing of characters is merely a symptom of the laziness and
contempt for their vehicle that is the too usual hall-mark of the
English writer of nuvvles. And that it should be tremendously
applauded is a symptom of the disdain that the English critic
really feels for the novel. If English painting consisted of nothing
but the caricatures of Rowlandson, Gilray, or Cruikshank the art-
critic would discover very soon that that grew monotonous, but
since it is merely a matter of prose-fiction it is easily accepted as
good enough; that which is too stupid to be said in any other way
being consigned to the novel. * * *

And the trouble with the English nuvvelist from Fielding to
Meredith is that not one of them cares whether you quite believe
in their characters or not. If you had told Flaubert or Conrad in
the midst of their passionate composings that you were not convinced of the reality of Homais or Tuan Jim as like as not they
would have called you out and shot you and in similar circumstances Richardson would have shewed himself extremely disagreeable. But Fielding, Thackeray, or Meredith would have
cared relatively little about that, though any one of them would
have knocked you down if they could, supposing you had sug-

gested that he was not a 'gentleman.' So would any English novelist today.

That of course is admirable in its effect on Anglo-Saxon literary-social life where anyone taking pen in hand becomes ipso facto an esquire for all users of type-writing machines. But it is bitter bad for the English novel.

It is bitter bad for the English novel because—as is the case with all human enterprises—the art of the novel is so difficult a thing that unless a man's whole energies are given to it he had much better otherwise occupy himself. For if Shakespeare's ambitions for coat-armour had antedated instead of coming after *The Tempest* where should we be today? We have to thank our stars that he was first a lousy, adulterous, poaching scoundrel—like Villon!

The lot of the novelist is in fact, hard—but not harder than that of any other man. If you put it to bakers, tram-conductors, politicians, or musicians that they must be first bakers and the rest and then gentlemen they will sigh, but admit it. It is almost only the English novelist who will aspire at being first gentleman and then craftsman—or even not craftsman at all since it is not really gentlemanly to think of being anything but a gentleman.

This is an incisive way of putting a truth that might perhaps be more wrapped up in social or material generalizations, but it is none the less a hard truth, and if you consider the case of Fielding, connected with the best families, placeman and diplomatist in a small way and compare him with Smollett who was socially nothing at all with no chance of a change you will see that truth all the more clearly.

God forbid that I should say anything really condemnatory of any book by any brother-novelist alive or dead. One is here to commend all that one can commend and to leave the rest alone. But there are few books that I more cordially dislike than *Tom Jones*. This is no critical pronouncement but merely a statement of a personal prejudice: one may dislike grape-fruit and yet acknowledge its admirable qualities, or one may, as I do, dislike the quality of gooseflesh that reading Mr. George Moore will confer on one's skin and yet acknowledge Mr. Moore as easily the greatest of living technicians.

But as regards *Tom Jones* my personal dislike goes along with a certain coldblooded, critical condemnation. I dislike Tom Jones, the character, because he is a lewd, stupid, and treacherous phenomenon; I dislike Fielding, his chronicler, because he is a bad sort of hypocrite. Had Fielding been in the least genuine in his moral aspirations it is Blifil that he would have painted attractively and Jones who would have come to the electric chair as would have been the case had Jones lived today.

Of course that is merely saying that Fielding liked a type that I dislike—but what appals me in view of the serious, cynical foreigner that I have postulated our taking about with us is the extremely thin nature of all the character-drawing, of all the events and of all the catastrophes. Is it to be seriously believed that Tom Jones's benefactor would have turned upon him on the flimsy nature of the evidence adduced against him or, equally, is it to be believed that Tom Jones's young woman would have again taken up with him after all the eye-openers she had had, she being represented as a girl of spirit? It simply isn't in any world of any seriousness at all. The fact, in short is, that Tom Jones is a papier mâché figure, the catastrophes, the merest invention without any pretence at being convincing and even the mere morality of the most leering and disastrous kind.

For myself, I am no moralist: I consider that if you do what you want you must take what you get for it and that if you deny yourself things you will be better off than if you don't. But fellows like Fielding, and to some extent Thackeray, who pretend that if you are a gay drunkard, lecher, squanderer of your goods and fumbler in placket-holes you will eventually find a benevolent uncle, concealed father or benefactor who will shower on you bags of tens of thousands of guineas, estates and the hands of adorable mistresses—those fellows are dangers to the body-politic and horribly bad constructors of plots.

It is all very well to say that such happy endings were the convention of the day, that you find them in the *School for Scandal*, the *Vicar of Wakefield* and in every eighteenth century romance that you pick up out of the twopenny book-box and it is all very well to say that the public demands a happy ending. But the really great writer is not bound by the conventions of his day, nor, if he desires to give his reader a happy ending need he select a wastrel like Jones as the recipient of his too easily bestowed favours.

If, in short, we are to regard Fielding as a serious writer writing for grown-up people we must regard him also as a rather intolerable scoundrel with perhaps *Jonathan Wild* to his credit. But *Jonathan Wild* is of another category and, neither winking nor leering, might be regarded as the finger on the wall, pointing out what happens to the Tom Joneses of the world if their case is regarded with any seriousness.

But the fact is that for a century and a half after the death of Fielding nothing in the Anglo-Saxon world was further from anyone, either novelist or layman, than the idea that the novel could be taken seriously. It was a thing a little above a fairy-tale for children, a little above a puppet-play; and, if not actually as damned socially and clerically as the actor who could not be either received at court or buried in consecrated ground, the novelist was practically without what the French call an *état civil* because his was not a serious profession. In England that state of things still pertains. In the demobilization forms after the late war the novelist was actually placed in the eighteenth category— along with gipsies, vagrants, and other non-productive persons; and my last public act in Great Britain being to allow my name to be placed on a list of voters, when I gave my avocation to the political agent as being that of a novelist, he exclaimed: "Oh, don't say that, sir. Say 'Gentleman'!" He was anxious that his list should appear as serious as possible.

That being the state of things and the novelist being human— for you cannot be a novelist and lack the ordinary aspirations of the human being!—for that century and a half the Anglo-Saxon public had the novels that it deserved. I do not mean to say that generous spirits lacked amongst the ranks of fiction-writers. That great genius, Dickens, thrashed oppressions and shams with the resplendent fury of an Isaiah and that singular megalomaniac,

Charles Reade, did, with *It Is Never Too Late to Mend,* really succeed in modifying the system of solitary confinement in English gaols. And you have had *Uncle Tom's Cabin.* But those works of propaganda had either no literary value at all or when, as in the case of Dickens they did have the literary value that genius can infuse into work however faulty, their work itself suffered by the very intensity of their reforming passions. * * *

In the meantime, across the Channel, the main stream of the Novel pursued its slow course.

It had begun with Richardson. His vogue with the French would be incomprehensible if we were not able to consider that the French Revolution was, in the end, a sentimental movement, basing itself on civic, parental, filial, and rhetorical virtues. If the French beheaded Marie Antoinette it was in order that Monsieur Durand, stay-maker of the Passage Choiseul might be sufficiently well-fed to utter tearful homilies to his children; for homilies uttered by starving peasants with their bones pushing through their skins and rags—such homilies would little impress their children with the solid advantages of virtuous careers. And the moment you consider pre-revolutionary France from that angle the appeal of the author of *Pamela* becomes instantly blindingly clear.

At any rate, Diderot wrote *Rameau's Nephew* as a direct imitation of that work of Richardson and a whole school of the contemporaries of Diderot imitated *Rameau's Nephew.* The influence, again, of Richardson is plainly visible in Chateaubriand—for without Richardson how could he have written long passages like: "How sad it is to think that eyes that are too old to see have not yet outlived the ability to shed tears," and the like. And if the Richardsonian influence upon Stendhal does not so immediately spring to the eye we know from Stendhal's letters that it was extremely profound.

It was to Diderot—and still more to Stendhal—that the Novel owes its next great step forward. That consisted in the discovery that words put into the mouth of a character need not be considered as having the personal backing of the author. At that point it became suddenly evident that the Novel as such was capable of being regarded as a means of profoundly serious and many-sided discussion and therefore a medium of profoundly serious investigation into the human case. It came into its own.

It is obvious of course that before the day of Diderot authors had put into the mouths of their characters sentiments with which they themselves could not be imagined to sympathize. But that was done only by characters marked "villain," all the sympathetic characters having to utter sentiments which were either those of the author or those with which the author imagined the solid middle-classes would agree. Young Mr. Blifil, Mrs. Slipslop, and the rest might say very wicked things but they were so obviously wicked and absurd that no one could take them with any seriousness either as pronouncements or as anything that could be taken as the author's opinion: Mr. Allworthy or Amelia Dobbin on the other hand could never utter anything without the reader having to exclaim: *"How* virtuous!" . . . And consider the material success that always awaited the good!

By the time the thirty years or so that stretched between 1790 and 1820 had impinged on the world it had gradually become evident, on the Continent at least, that so many differing codes of morality could synchronize in the same era, in the same nation and even in the same small community—it had become so evident that if Simeon Stylites and Oliver Cromwell were saints, Jesus Christ and Gautama Buddha and several Chinese philosophers were very good men, that the Novel, if it was at all to express its day must express itself through figures less amateurishly blacked than Uriah Heep and less sedulously whited than the Cheryble brothers. * * *

So with *Le Rouge et le Noir* it became evident to the world that the novel of discussion or of investigation was a possibility and, with that discovery, the great novels began to come. The discussions to be found in the very few works of fiction by Diderot were naturally experimental and amateurish. Like Richardson he was tremendously on the side of the more or less patriarchal and civic angels. Nevertheless he could give you a parasite talking in favour of his profession or a rogue justifying his courses with a sincerity and a reasonable ingenuousness that differed extremely from the exaggerated speeches of the villains of the Fielding, the Dickens, or the commercial nuvvle, schools. Stendhal on the other hand being what one might call a cold Nietzschean—or it might be more just to say that Nietzsche was a warmed up Stendhalean —Stendhal, then, swung the balance rather to the other extreme, tending to make his detrimentals argumentatively masterly and his conventionally virtuous characters banal and impotent.

At any rate, with or after Stendhal, it became evident that, if the novel was to have what is called *vraisemblance,* if it was so to render life as to engross its reader, the novelist must not take sides either with the virtuous whose virtues cause them to prosper or with the vicious whose very virtues drive them always nearer and nearer to the gallows or the pauper's grave. That does not say that the author need abstain from letting his conventionally virtuous characters prosper to any thinkable extent. For however scientifically the matter be considered, material if not intellectual honesty, sobriety, continence, frugality, parsimony, and the other material virtues will give any man a better chance of fourteen thousand—pounds or dollars—a year than if he should be, however intellectually honest, financially unsound, or a drunkard or a dreamer or one who never talks about the baths he takes. The publisher, in fact, has a better chance of both terrestrial and skyey mansions than the novelist. * * *

It was Flaubert who most shiningly preached the doctrine of the novelist as Creator who should have a Creator's aloofness, rendering the world as he sees it, uttering no comments, falsifying no issues and carrying the subject—the Affair—he has selected for rendering, remorselessly out to its logical conclusion.

There came thus into existence the novel of Aloofness. It had even in France something of a struggle for that existence and the author of *Madame Bovary* which was the first great novel logically—and indeed passionately—to carry out this theory, had to face a criminal prosecution because in the opinion of the government of Napoleon III a book that is not actively on the side of constituted authority and of established morality is of necessity dangerous to morals and subversive of good government.

That view—it is still largely entertained by the academic crit-

ics of Anglo-Saxondom—is of course imbecile but it is not without
a certain basis in the sentiments of common humanity. It is normal for poor, badgered men to desire to read of a sort of representative type who, as hero of a book, shall triumph over all
obstacles with surprising ease and as if with the backing of a
deity. In that way they can dream of easy ends for themselves.
So they will dislike authors who do not side with their own types.
And as constituted governments and academic bodies are made
up of what the French call *hommes moyen sensuels* such corpora-
tions will do what they can to prevent novelists from not taking
sides with agreeable characters.

To the theory of Aloofness added itself, by a very natural
process, the other theory that the story of a novel should be the
history of an Affair and not the invention of a tale in which a
central character with an attendant female should be followed
through a certain space of time until the book comes to a happy
end on a note of matrimony or to an unhappy end—represented
by a death. That latter—the normal practice of the earlier novelist
and still the normal expedient of the novel of commerce or of
escape—is again imbecile, but again designed to satisfy a very
natural human desire for finality. We have a natural desire to be
kidded into thinking that for nice agreeable persons like ourselves
life will finally bring us to a stage where an admirably planned
villa, a sempiternally charming—and yet changing—companion,
and a sufficiency of bathrooms, automobiles, gramophones, radios,
and grand pianos to establish us well in the forefront of the class
to which we hope to belong shall witness the long, uneventful,
fortunate and effortless closing years of our lives. And our desire
to be kidded into that belief is all the stronger in that whenever
we do examine with any minuteness into the lives of our fellow
human beings practically nothing of the sort ever happens to
them. So we say: "Life is too sad for us to want to read books
that remind us of it!"

But that is the justification for the novel of Aloofness, rendering not the arbitrary felicities of a central character but the
singular normalities of an Affair. Normal humanity, deprived of
the possibility of viewing either lives or life, makes naturally for

a pessimism that demands relief either in the drugs of the happy endings of falsified fictions or in the anodynes of superstition—one habit being as fatal to the human intelligence as the other. But there is no need to entertain the belief that life is sad any more than there is any benefit to be derived from the contemplation of fictitious and banal joys. The French peasant long ago evolved the rule that life is never either as good or as bad as one expects it to be and so the French peasant, like every proper man, faces life with composure—and reads *Madame Bovary* whilst the English, say, lawyer has never got beyond the *Three Musketeers*.

The progress from the one to the other is simple and logical enough. If you no longer allow yourself to take sides with your characters you begin very soon to see that such a thing as a hero does not exist—a discovery that even Thackeray could make. And, from there to seeing that it is not individuals that succeed or fail but enterprises or groups that do is a very small step to take. And then immediately there suggests itself the other fact that it is not the mere death and still less the mere marriage of an individual that brings to an end either a group or an enterprise. It is perhaps going too far to say that *no* man is indispensable but it is far more usual to find that, when a seemingly indispensable individual disappears for one reason or another from an enterprise, that adventure proceeds with equanimity and very little shock. * * *

Flaubert, then, gave us *Madame Bovary* which may be described as the first great novel that aimed at aloofness. That it did not succeed in its aim, Flaubert being in the end so fascinated by his Emma that beside her and the ingenuous weakness of her genuine romanticism every other character in the book is either hypocritical, mean or meanly imbecile—that it did not succeed in that aim is not to be wondered at when we consider the great, buoyant, and essentially optimist figure that he was. And indeed, all authors being men, it is very unlikely that the completely aloof novel will ever see the light. If you want to be a novelist you must first be a poet and it is impossible to be a poet and lack human sympathies or generosity of outlook. In *Education Sentimentale*—which, if I had to decide the matter which fortunately I don't, I should call the greatest novel ever written—the author of *Madame Bovary* gave us a nearly perfect group novel, written from a standpoint of very nearly complete aloofness. In *Bouvard et Pecuchet*, abandoning as it were human measures of success and failure, he takes as his hero the imbecility of co-operative mankind and as his heroine the futility of the accepted idea, and, being thus as it were detached from the earth and its standards, he could draw in Bouvard and his mate, two of the most lovable of human beings that ever set out upon a forlorn hope. He died in the attempt.

The Flaubert school or group lasted sufficiently long in France though, after the late war its influence was completely washed out by a sort of eclecticism whose main features it is very difficult to trace and into whose ramifications I do not intend to enter for it has had practically no time to influence the work of Anglo-Saxon novel writers. Flaubert, Maupassant, Turgenev, the Gourmonts, Daudet, and the rest of those who had their places at Brébant's died in their allotted years, the last survivor of any prominence being Anatole France whose death was greeted by an outburst of furious hatred in France such as can seldom have greeted the passing of a distinguished figure. That was because the French young, saddened and rendered starving by the war which just preceded France's death turned with loathing from the rather debonnaire aloofness of the author of *Histoire Comique*. And indeed if we Anglo-Saxons had suffered in the least as much as those Latins I might well expect to find myself lynched for writing what I have done above. I have seldom witnessed anything to equal the dismay of a great French gathering of littérateurs when their honoured guest, an English novelist of distinction and indeed of internationally public literary functions told them in quite immaculate French that all he knew of writing he had from France, and that all that he had from France he had learned from the works of Guy de Maupassant! If he had gone round that great assembly and had, with his glove, flicked each one of the guests in the face, he could not have caused greater consternation. Nevertheless it is true that Maupassant must have had more influence on the Anglo-Saxon writer of today than any other writer of fiction, Henry James possibly excepted.

Ford Madox Ford, *The English Novel, From the Earliest Days to the Death of Joseph Conrad* (Philadelphia and London: J. B. Lippincott Co., 1929), pp. 78–91, 121–124, 126–128, 129–133, 135–137.

The Reader

In 1924 Ford founded in Paris a literary journal called The Transatlantic Review. *Receiving from the first the enthusiastic support of Ezra Pound and Gertrude Stein, it also published the work of James Joyce, Ernest Hemingway, and E. E. Cummings. Although financial difficulties prevented it from continuing for more than a year, it contributed largely to the revival of Anglo-Saxon literature which was centered in Paris during the 1920's. In addition to publishing the works of young writers, the* Transatlantic *was used by Ford as a means of reassessing literary standards. It therefore contained a series of pseudonymous articles called "Stocktaking" which were designed to encourage a revaluation of the function of English literature in the post-war era.*

The essay printed below is one of this series, and is of particular value insofar as it deals with a basic concern of literary endeavor, namely its acceptance by the public. Adopting, as he so often did, an autobiographical approach, Ford in this piece concentrates on the function of literature and the meaning it has for mankind.

Let it be granted that a re-valuation of English—of all Anglo-Saxon—Literature is a thing eminently to be desired; and few indeed are those who will deny that it is desirable. Their point of view, their reasons for the desire would differ widely, some, amongst whom would be the Reader, I hope, and certainly the Writer, desiring that, so re-valued and trumpeted with enthusiasm by great nations, English letters may take their place again amongst the literatures of the world; some desiring to insulate still further the printed matter of Anglo Saxondom, restoring it to the "English" tradition of writers like De Quincey, Oliver Wendell Holmes, Henry Wadsworth Longfellow, James Russell

Lowell, Charles Lamb, Alexander Montgomery, Lords Macaulay, Tennyson and Lytton, whom the European will not very willingly read; and others again—and they the great majority perhaps amongst Deans—being determined to the best of their abilities, since writing has been exhausted in the practices of the long line of Anglican Divines from Archbishop Cranmer to the late Mr. Spurgeon,—being determined then to abolish the reading of all works of the imagination. . . . In short there are an infinite number of reasons for desiring a re-estimation of our literary values. . . .

I was sitting in the dusk, last Spring, in a hardly defined London room, awaiting the return from business of the master of the house. It was truly what is called the owlight! But with a book upon his knee, in a window-seat, his back to the dusky panes was a young boy—say he was sixteen. He did not stir; I did not speak for a long time.

I had asked him what was the name of the book and he had answered: "Oh, Goldsmith . . . *The Deserted Village.*" and I had got from him, rather painfully, the information that he being waiting for a scholarship exam had got up the names and dates of Oliver Goldsmith amongst a list of English Writers of the Eighteenth Century. Seeing Goldsmith's *Deserted Village* on his father's bookshelves he had taken it down—for the first time in how many years?

I pestered him with no more questions: I was the casual adult in the house, say a not very esteemed uncle; he was the master of all us writers. He was the Reader!

I had nearly written: He was the Only Reader. For there is no reading like that of a boy in the long dusks: it is the deepest abandonment of the soul that we know on this earth . . . But his father came in after a long time and began to chide him for wasting his time when he should be reading for his examination and he took up a German dictionary and a manual of biology and went into another room. The father said that if the boy would only read something useful he would be less worried. And then he began to upbraid *me* for writing disrespectfully of Shelley, an English Classic. He said he had been told that I was hurting my reputation. Truly the ways of both writers and Readers are thorny ways!

All the same I should not have chosen *The Deserted Village* in the days when I ruined my eyes with those long, twilight readings. My authors were Marryat; Scott, a little; Defoe, Lope da Vega; Hermann Alemannos—*Guzman d'Alfarache, Lazarillo de Tormes, Lorna Doone, Melmoth the Wanderer,* Gibbon's *Decline and Fall,* Robertson's *History of Charles V,* an odd volume of North's *Plutarch,* an odd volume of Landor's *Imaginary Conversations* containing the conversation between Leofric and Godiva; naturally also *Hark-Away Dick, Sweeny Todd, the Demon Barber; The Scalp-Hunters; Westward Ho!* which upon consideration seems to me to be the most wicked book ever written, and Dean Farrar's *Eric* which is perhaps the next most wicked—or less, or more.

I suppose almost every human being could compile a similar list and the exercise is a fascinating one. But I am not writing biography—or only concealedly!—so I will leave the matter there, harping merely on the fact that those were the books I found engrossing. I could read most of them over and over again and indeed often enough I would turn straight back to the first leaf as soon as I had come to the last. I remember making a note in a schoolboy's pocket book that on such a date—I fancy it was the 17/12/(18)86—I had read Lorna Doone thirteen times: I can still relate whole passages of it by heart. But I *will* delay a moment to pay a tribute to what I thought then—and I think it still—*sui generis* the most beautiful book in the world: Samuel Smiles' *Life of a Scottish Naturalist.* I found this book by chance a year ago, bought it for sixpence and recognised at once that my intimate cadence, the typical sentence that I try all my life to create, that I hear all the while in my ear and only once in a blue moon am aided to write, is to be found always in the recorded speeches of Thomas Edward. His sentences have a dying fall, a cadence of resignation. He will write of dotterels on the wet sands, of spoonbills labouring in the immense engineering feat of turning over a great dead fish, of foxes in their homes on the faces of the sea-cliffs—and it is as if you were hearing a *nunc dimittis* spoken without pomp or self-consciousness. Only once did he—as far as Smiles' records go—did he utter a *Jubilate*: he had fallen over a precipice and, caught by a projecting shelf, with his ribs smashed, unable to move and with no apparent prospect of succour, he was enabled to observe an osprey devouring a partridge on a near-by crag. He utters a paean of praise at sight of the beauty, the noble ferocity and address of the bird, and then, thanking the Creator for permitting him to see what perhaps no other man had ever been permitted to witness, this journeyman cobbler who never in his life earned more than eighteen shillings a week, addresses himself to descending the crags . . .

But I cannot imagine myself, as a young boy, reading *The Deserted Village,* and that must have been a matter of choice for almost certainly it fell under my attention. I was permitted the run of one—of several!—extensive if heterogeneous collections of books and I had most of my dusks to myself. And I remember the proprietor of the first private school to which I was sent at the age of eight or ten telling me that, he having written to my father to ask whether at home I was really permitted to read all the books I seemed to have read, my father had answered that he wished me to have the run of all the books in the schoolmaster's house but would prefer me not to read "Byron."

I naturally dipped into Byron: what boy would not have? But I never read more than a line or two and I can remember now with exactitude the sensations that that line or two then caused me. It was at once a weariness, a sort of reluctant dread and a sense as of intense repletion as if after an already too heavy meal I had been confronted with a large quantity of something sweet. And indeed I have the foreshadowings of all those sensations still whenever I look at an opened volume with the columns of verse that seem to have come already many weary miles beyond the left hand page and to be going on for leagues and leagues after the bottom of the right hand page has been reached. I believe that the greater part of humanity feels like that and that that is why the Epic is no longer very fashionable. The reason, I daresay, lies in the personality one ascribes to the writers of immense poems: one imagines them to have uncontemplatable

industries, seriousnesses that appal, minatory features—every kind
of portentousness. And since the greater part of life is passed,
whether one like it or no, in being overborne by one portentousness or another, one will not very willingly let oneself be similarly
overwhelmed in the course of an operation which should be a
matter of freewill at least, if not of pleasure. I do not mean that I
was assailed by those thoughts when as a boy I opened the *Deserted Village*. It was probably something else that stopped me
when I had read no more than; (I quote from memory)

> Dear lovely bow'rs of Innocence and Ease,
> Seats of my Youth when every sport could please,
> How often have I loitered o'er thy green
> Where humble happiness endeared each scene!
> How often have I gazed on every charm,
> The sheltered cot, the cultivated farm,
> The never-failing brook, the busy mill,
> The decent Church that topped the neighb'ring Hill!

I remember to this day saying to myself:

"Why couldn't the fellow have written: *I have loitered on
thy green: I have gazed upon thy charm,*" instead of asking with
a note of exclamation questions that can have no possible answer
and can be meant to have none. And "Innocence and Ease" made
me feel impatient at once. And that was not because I had not
patience. I owe it to the long London twilights of those years
that I can say I have read every word of *Artaxerxes,* every word
of *Guzman d'Alfarache,* every word of the *Castle of Otranto,*
every word of the *Man of Feeling.* For the matter of that, even
in later years I have read every word of Mr. Doughty's *Dawn in
Britain*—and that with enthusiasm! I do not imagine that any
living soul other than myself can claim *all* those endurances.

So I will not confess to any abnormal lack of patience: nevertheless I could not do, and I never could have done what that
young boy was doing for his own pleasure and with such engrossment. Anyhow, there we have the Readers; I am tempted to say
the Two Readers. For humanity seems to divine itself into two
types when it comes to reading: Those who like particularisations
and shun allegories and those who reverse the processes of liking

and avoiding. There will, that is to say, be those who will desire
to read of Villages distinguished by bow'rs of Innocence and Ease;
there will be those who, comfortably and with engrossment, can
only read of such a village as:

> The village of Selborne and large hamlet of Oakhanger, with the
> single farms, and many scattered houses along the verge of the forest,
> contain upwards of six hundred and seventy inhabitants. We abound
> with poor; many of whom are sober and industrious, and live comfort-
> ably" (Oh bow'rs of Innocence and Ease!) "in good stone or brick cot-
> tages which are glazed and have chambers above stairs: mud buildings
> we have none ... The inhabitants enjoy a good share of health and
> longevity: and the parish swarms with children.

One is tempted to say that it is the eighteenth century against
the twentieth were it not for the fact that the letters which make
up the *Natural History of Selborne* were being written long before
and were continued long after the "composition" of the *Deserted
Village*. Still it is fair to put it that White's *Selborne* attracted
very little attention in the eighteenth century and is very much
read nowadays whereas the *Deserted Village* must have found
very few to read it for pleasure or interest during the last fifty
years. It may have been "set" for examinations or eighteenth-
century-minded pastors and masters may have enjoined its perusal
as a virtue and so it may have found readers who desired to
improve themselves. But it can hardly have been much read
either as part of the literature of escape or as a work to which
nineteenth-to-twentieth century writers have gone for a model.

But about these things there is no finality and the very fact
that that boy, like myself, at his age a boy normal enough, should
find engrossment in Goldsmith's poem may well be a sign of a reaction towards the Allegory of the eighteenth, or even towards
the Great Moral Purpose of the mid-nineteenth, centuries. Quite
apart from the fashionable taste in literatures being a matter of
endless reactions, the Literature of Escape itself, the beloved and
engrossing printed matter that we read at dusk, is probably in
the nature of a re-action against our surroundings. Indeed it is
assuredly that and nothing else, the typewriting-girl desiring to
read works in which typewriting-girls all marry their employers

of the merchant sea-man in the fo'csle—and they are the most avid readers of all—desiring only books in which, please God, there shall be no more sea. We want to get away from our debts.

So the Allegory may well come into its own again and flourish even as it does on the base of the Albert Memorial where a gentleman in a frock-coat carrying a test-tube typifies Science; a nude figure leading a zebu-bull, the Colonies; a lady with a nondescriptly rigged ship beneath her arm, the Dominion of the Seas; and the gilt figure of Albert the Good, the Prince of Peace. There may well be conditions in our time to make the weary soul desire to get away into that sort of thing. And indeed the portents are not lacking!

In the more official school of literary Company Promoter of to-day the tendency is avowedly to bring back the "English tradition" and indeed the tendency is not limited to the official school which in England is purely Whig. Only to-day, looking through the pages of a fashionable Tory organ I came upon a review of a volume of poems that still leaves me wondering whether it is not meant to pull the leg of someone or other. It purports to

bring to the notice of our readers one of the most extraordinary volumes of poems published for a generation.... Alone among the younger poets Mr. . . . restores to English poetry the larger virtues, the grand manner . . .

"He swings his boat away
"Even as a lonely thinker who has run
"The gamut of great lore and found the Inane" . . .

Philosophy influences his blood like a sensuous excitement, the exalted, impersonal business of States is more his theme than any personal pre-occupation.

Another quotation ends with the singular line:

England arisen, bared for the battle, blows!

I suppose Macaulay's review of Satan Montgomery contains citations of lines more comic, but then Macaulay did not regard Montgomery as a saviour of society.

Perhaps however it is all a joke. Or perhaps it isn't: there may be Readers—there may be thousands, whole millions of Readers to whom the figure of England blowing may indeed be sublime. The thought opens out for contemplation an immense vista. At the end of it, as through the small end of a prophetic telescope, the Man of Business at the railway bookstall as he goes down town. He wears a full wig, a purple velvet coat, ruffles and a sword and with a gesture of horror he says to the bookstall clerk:

"Take away that Daily . . . Bring to me, boy, the last sublime epic of the immortal So and So!"

That is not fanciful: it is a perfectly logical projection supposing that the official critic of to-day should have his way—or supposing merely that the swing or the pendulum should still, as it always has, prevail. Nor is it one half so fanciful as a faithful projection of ourselves, going down town to-day and faced on the bookstall with the incredible rubbish that is all that there you will find—would have seemed to Dr. Johnson! For, if there is a pendulum to swing—and almost certainly there is!—it goes to and fro between the awful state of the Full Wig and the sceptical mobility of the Rag Time Army that to-day we are. Or that yesterday we were!

For, certainly, between 1914 and 1919 such a line as:

"England bared for the battle, blows" would have excited little enthusiasm: would have cut no ice anywhere at all! Indeed it is hardly likely that in those days we were even moved by the remembrance of the great precursor of that sort of thing:

> So when an angel by divine command
> With rising tempests shakes a guilty land,
> Such as of late o'er pale Britannia past,
> Calm and serene he drives the furious blast;
> And pleased th'Almighty's orders to perform
> Rides in the whirlwind and directs the storm!

In a Division with which I was acquainted we used to say:

"Pore . . . . . y old Plumer's got 'em on the run!" And it meant the same as was meant by Addison, but it took less time to say. Indeed, viewed philosophically, you may put it that the whole of the late Armageddon was caused by antagonism between

the one point of view and the other: it was the pip-squeak not 'arf
against the Shining Sword; Mr. Kipling's banjo against the
Addisonian lyre. And inasmuch as most of our Academic-Official
criticism is and must of necessity be produced by gentleman
temperamentally and ingrainedly pro-German it stands to reason
that the object of their work will be to restore the Allegory and
with it the dreadful Lives of Poets, the annotated editions, kai
panta tauta. I deplore the prospect, for, as the Reader will no
doubt have divined I am for the banjo against the lyre all the
time; for that is to say the natural man with appetites, desires,
physical aptitudes, carelessnesses and interests in life; as against
the Professorial Figure that stands for uninspired industry, career-
makings and circumspection: I desire that is to say that things
should be written, not written about. I deplore then the state
into which it is hoped to push this country; but I cannot help
seeing that it is extremely likely that into it she will be pushed . . .

Between Realism and the Allegoric stands however the Romantic: between, that is to say, Pope and Flaubert stands Victor
Hugo; between the eighteenth and the twentieth, another century! And it is quite possible that in Anglo-Saxondom a cleavage
will come and that, whilst England returns to its diet of half-cold
fish—at any rate on the surface, the United States may produce
and immensely consume an immense, hybrid Romantic-Realist
literature. For it is obvious that the United States with its mixed
populations is not going to be limited or turned back to the diet
provided by the Concord Group which represents the last activities of the "English" muse in America: ever since the days of
Mark Twain and Whitman, and still more of Stephen Crane, it
was quite obvious that America was going to have a literature of
her own—and a literature nearer in spirit to the literature of the
Continent than to the literature of the "Mother Country."

"Daniel Chaucer" (pseud. Ford Madox Ford), "Stocktaking. Towards a
Re-Valuation of English Literature—X. 'The Reader'," *The Transatlantic Review* II, 5 (October 1924), 502–510.

IMPRESSIONISM AND FICTION

On Impressionism

By 1913, when the following article was published, Ford had become a novelist of some prominence in England and was about to demonstrate, in The Good Soldier, *the degree to which he had mastered the fictional methods he himself believed in. Thus this essay is an assessment of the techniques which, both by himself and in collaboration with Joseph Conrad, he had labored so long to master.*

The word Impressionism had been widely used to characterize the school of novelists to which Ford and Conrad both belonged. Clearly deriving its label from that applied to French painters like Monet, the school wished neither to follow Zola's sociological approach to reality, nor to use the artificial patterns of the plotted Victorian novel to achieve the essence of the real. They believed, rather, that this essence was to be captured only by a careful selection of telling detail and a concentration on the seemingly casual aspects of human relationships which so often, as in real life, provide true insights into personal relationships and human activities. Above all, it depended on visual information, which meant that the Impressionist could not tell the reader what was going on, either internally or externally. Instead, he had to show the reader these things.

This essay, first printed in two installments in Poetry and Drama, *was Ford's first extended treatment of his own methods as a novelist.*

I

These are merely some notes towards a working guide to Impressionism as a literary method.

I do not know why I should have been especially asked to write about Impressionism; even as far as literary Impressionism goes I claim no Papacy in the matter. A few years ago, if anybody had called me an Impressionist I should languidly have denied that I was anything of the sort or that I knew anything about the school, if there could be said to be any school. But one person and another in the last ten years has called me Impressionist with such persistence that I have given up resistance. I don't know; I just write books, and if someone attaches a label to me I do not much mind.

I am not claiming any great importance for my work; I daresay it is all right. At any rate, I am a perfectly self-conscious writer; I know exactly how I get my effects, as far as those effects go. Then, if I am in truth an Impressionist, it must follow that a conscientious and exact account of how I myself work will be an account, from the inside, of how Impressionism is reached, produced, or gets its effects. I can do no more.

This is called egotism; but, to tell the truth, I do not see how Impressionism can be anything else. Probably this school differs from other schools, principally, in that it recognises, frankly, that all art must be the expression of an ego, and that if Impressionism is to do anything, it must, as the phrase is, go the whole hog. The difference between the description of a grass by the agricultural correspondent of the *Times* newspaper and the description of the same grass by Mr W. H. Hudson is just the difference—the measure of the difference between the egos of the two gentlemen. The difference between the description of any given book by a sound English reviewer and the description of the same book by some foreigner attempting Impressionist criticism is again merely a matter of the difference in the ego.

Mind, I am not saying that the non-Impressionist productions may not have their values—their very great values. The Impressionist gives you his own views, expecting you to draw deductions, since presumably you know the sort of chap he is. The agricultural correspondent of the *Times,* on the other hand—and a jolly good writer he is—attempts to give you, not so much his own impressions of a new grass as the factual observations of himself and of as many as possible other sound authorities. He will tell you how many blades of the new grass will grow upon an acre, what height they will attain, what will be a reasonable tonnage to expect when green, when sun-dried in the form of hay or as ensilage. He will tell you the fattening value of the new fodder in its various forms and the nitrogenous value of the manure dropped by the so-fattened beasts. He will provide you, in short, with reading that is quite interesting to the layman, since all facts are interesting to men of good will; and the agriculturist he will provide with information of real value. Mr Hudson, on the other hand, will give you nothing but the pleasure of coming in contact with his temperament, and I doubt whether, if you read with the greatest care his description of false sea-buckthorn (*hippophae rhamnoides*) you would very willingly recognise that greenish-grey plant, with the spines and the berries like reddish amber, if you came across it.

Or again—so at least I was informed by an editor the other day—the business of a sound English reviewer is to make the readers of the paper understand exactly what sort of a book it is that the reviewer is writing about. Said the editor in question: "You have no idea how many readers your paper will lose if you employ one of those brilliant chaps who write readable articles about books. You will get yourself deluged with letter after letter from subscribers saying they have bought a book on the strength of articles in your paper; that the book isn't in the least what they expected, and that therefore they withdraw their subscriptions." What the sound English reviewer, therefore, has to do is to identify himself with the point of view of as large a number of readers of the journal for which he may be reviewing, as he can easily do, and then to give them as many facts about the book under consideration as his allotted space will hold. To do this he must sacrifice his personality, and the greater part of his readability. But he will probably very much help his editor, since the great majority of readers do not want to read anything that any reasonable person would want to read; and they do not want to come into contact with the personality of the critic, since they have obviously never been introduced to him.

The ideal critic, on the other hand—as opposed to the so-exemplary reviewer—is a person who can so handle words that from the first three phrases any intelligent person—any foreigner, that is to say, and any one of three inhabitants of these islands—any intelligent person will know at once the sort of chap that he is dealing with. Letters of introduction will therefore be unnecessary, and the intelligent reader will know pretty well what sort of book the fellow is writing about because he will know the sort of fellow the fellow is. I don't mean to say that he would necessarily trust his purse, his wife, or his mistress to the Impressionist critic's care. But that is not absolutely necessary. The ambition, however, of my friend the editor was to let his journal give the impression of being written by those who could be trusted with the wives and purses—not, of course, the mistresses, for there would be none—of his readers.

You will, perhaps, be beginning to see now what I am aiming at—the fact that Impressionism is a frank expression of personality; the fact that non-Impressionism is an attempt to gather together the opinions of as many reputable persons as may be and to render them truthfully and without exaggeration. (The Impressionist must always exaggerate.)

II

Let us approach this matter historically—as far as I know anything about the history of Impressionism, though I must warn you that I am a shockingly ill-read man. Here, then, are some examples: do you know, for instance, Hogarth's drawing of the watchman with the pike over his shoulder and the dog at his heels going in at a door, the whole being executed in four lines? Here it is:

Now, that is the high-watermark of Impressionism; since, if you look at those lines for long enough, you will begin to see the watchman with his slouch hat, the handle of the pike coming well down into the cobble-stones, the knee-breeches, the leathern garters strapped round his stocking, and the surly expression of the dog, which is bull-hound with a touch of mastiff in it.

You may ask why, if Hogarth saw all these things, did he not put them down on paper, and all that I can answer is that he made this drawing for a bet. Moreover why, if you can see all these things for yourself, should Hogarth bother to put them down on paper? You might as well contend that Our Lord ought to have delivered a lecture on the state of primary education in the Palestine of the year 32 or thereabouts, together with the statistics of rickets and other infantile diseases caused by neglect and improper feeding—a disquisition in the manner of Mrs Sidney Webb. He preferred, however, to say: "It were better that a millstone were put about his neck and he were cast into the deep sea." The statement is probably quite incorrect; the statutory punishment either here or in the next world has probably nothing to do with millstones and so on, but Our Lord was, you see, an Impressionist, and knew His job pretty efficiently. It is probable that He did not have access to as many Blue Books or white papers as the leaders of the Fabian Society, but, from His published utterances, one gathers that He had given a good deal of thought to the subject of children.

I am not in the least joking—and God forbid that I should be thought irreverent because I write like this. The point that I really wish to make is, once again, that—that the Impressionist gives you, as a rule, the fruits of his own observations and the fruits of his own observations alone. He should be in this as severe and as solitary as any monk. It is what he is in the world for. It is, for instance, not so much his business to quote as to state his impressions—that the Holy Scriptures are a good book, or a rotten book, or contain passages of good reading interspersed with dulness; or suggest gems in a cavern, the perfumes of aromatic woods burning in censers, or the rush of the feet of camels crossing the deep sands, or the shrill sounds of long trumpets

borne by archangels—clear sounds of brass like those in that
funny passage in "Aida."

The passage in prose, however, which I always take as a working model—and in writing this article I am doing no more than
showing you the broken tools and bits of oily rag which form my
brains, since once again I must disclaim writing with any authority on Impressionism—this passage in prose occurs in a story by
de Maupassant called *La Reine Hortense*. I spent, I suppose, a
great part of ten years in grubbing up facts about Henry VIII.
I worried about his parentage, his diseases, the size of his shoes,
the price he gave for kitchen implements, his relation to his
wives, his knowledge of music, his proficiency with the bow. I
amassed, in short, a great deal of information about Henry VIII.
I wanted to write a long book about him, but Mr Pollard, of the
British Museum, got the commission and wrote the book probably much more soundly. I then wrote three long novels all about
that Defender of the Faith. But I really know—so delusive are
reported facts—nothing whatever. Not one single thing! Should
I have found him affable, or terrifying, or seductive, or royal, or
courageous? There are so many contradictory facts; there are so
many reported interviews, each contradicting the other, so that
really all that I *know* about this king could be reported in the
words of Maupassant, which, as I say, I always consider as a
working model. Maupassant is introducing one of his characters,
who is possibly gross, commercial, overbearing, insolent; who
eats, possibly, too much greasy food; who wears commonplace
clothes—a gentleman about whom you might write volumes if
you wanted to give the facts of his existence. But all that de Maupassant finds it necessary to say is: "C'était un monsieur à favoris
rouges qui entrait toujours le premier."

And that is all that I *know* about Henry VIII.—that he was a
gentleman with red whiskers who always went first through a
door.

III

Let us now see how these things work out in practice. I have a
certain number of maxims, gained mostly in conversation with

Mr Conrad, which form my working stock-in-trade. I stick to them pretty generally; sometimes I throw them out of the window and just write whatever comes. But the effect is usually pretty much the same. I guess I must be fairly well drilled by this time and function automatically, as the Americans say. The first two of my maxims are these:

Always consider the impressions that you are making upon the mind of the reader, and always consider that the first impression with which you present him will be so strong that it will be all that you can ever do to efface it, to alter it or even quite slightly to modify it. Maupassant's gentleman with red whiskers, who always pushed in front of people when it was a matter of going through a doorway, will remain, for the mind of the reader, that man and no other. The impression is as hard and as definite as a tin-tack. And I rather doubt whether, supposing Maupassant represented him afterwards as kneeling on the ground to wipe the tears away from a small child who had lost a penny down a drain —I doubt whether such a definite statement of fact would ever efface the first impression from the reader's mind. They would think that the gentleman with the red whiskers was perpetrating that act of benevolence with ulterior motives—to impress the bystanders, perhaps.

Maupassant, however, uses physical details more usually as a method of introduction of this characters than I myself do. I am inclined myself, when engaged in the seductive occupation, rather to strike the keynote with a speech than with a description of personality, or even with an action. And, for that purpose, I should set it down, as a rule, that the first speech of a character you are introducing should always be a generalisation—since generalisations are the really strong indications of character. Putting the matter exaggeratedly, you might say that, if a gentleman sitting opposite you in the train remarked to you: "I see the Tories have won Leith Boroughs," you would have practically no guide to that gentleman's character. But, if he said: "Them bloody Unionists have crept into Leith because the Labourites, damn them, have taken away 1,100 votes from us," you would know that the gentleman belonged to a certain political party, had a certain social status, a certain degree of education and a certain amount of impatience.

It is possible that such disquisitions on Impressionism in prose fiction may seem out of place in a journal styled *Poetry and Drama*. But I do not think they are. For Impressionism, differing from other schools of art, is founded so entirely on observation of the psychology of the patron—and the psychology of the patron remains constant. Let me, to make things plainer, present you with a quotation. Sings Tennyson:

> And bats went round in fragrant skies,
>   And wheeled or lit the filmy shapes
>   That haunt the dusk, with ermine capes
> And woolly breasts and beady eyes.

Now that is no doubt very good natural history, but it is certainly not Impressionism, since no one watching a bat at dusk could see the ermine, the wool or the beadiness of the eyes. These things you might read about in books, or observe in the museum or at the Zoological Gardens. Or you might pick up a dead bat upon the road. But to import into the record of observations of one moment the observations of a moment altogether different is not Impressionism. For Impressionism is a thing altogether momentary.

I do not wish to be misunderstood. It is perfectly possible that the remembrance of a former observation may colour your impression of the moment, so that if Tennyson had said:

> And we remembered they have ermine capes,

he would have remained within the canons of Impressionism. But that was not his purpose, which, whatever it was, was no doubt praiseworthy in the extreme, because his heart was pure. It is, however, perfectly possible that a piece of Impressionism should give a sense of two, of three, of as many as you will, places, persons, emotions, all going on simultaneously in the emotions of the writer. It is, I mean, perfectly possible for a sensitised person, be he poet or prose writer, to have the sense, when he is in one room, that he is in another, or when he is speaking to one person he may be so intensely haunted by the memory or desire for another person that he may be absent-minded or distraught. And there is nothing in the canons of Impressionism, as I know it, to stop the attempt to render those superimposed emotions. Indeed, I suppose that Impressionism exists to render those queer effects of real life that are like so many views seen through bright glass—through glass so bright that whilst you perceive through it a landscape or a backyard, you are aware that, on its surface, it reflects a face of a person behind you. For the whole of life is really like that; we are almost always in one place with our minds somewhere quite other.

And it is, I think, only Impressionism that can render that peculiar effect; I know, at any rate, of no other method. It has, this school, in consequence, certain quite strong canons, certain quite rigid unities that must be observed. The point is that any piece of Impressionism, whether it be prose, or verse, or painting, or sculpture, is the record of the impression of a moment; it is not a sort of rounded, annotated record of a set of circumstances—it is the record of the recollection in your mind of a set of circumstances that happened ten years ago—or ten minutes. It might even be the impression of the moment—but it is the impression, not the corrected chronicle. I can make what I mean most clear by a concrete instance.

Thus an Impressionist in a novel, or in a poem, will never render a long speech of one of his characters verbatim, because the mind of the reader would at once lose some of the illusion of the good faith of the narrator. The mind of the reader will say: "Hullo, this fellow is faking this. He cannot possibly remember such a long speech word for word." The Impressionist, therefore, will only record his impression of a long speech. If you will try to remember what remains in your mind of long speeches you heard yesterday, this afternoon or five years ago, you will see what I mean. If to-day, at lunch at your club, you heard an irascible member making a long speech about the fish, what you remember will not be his exact words. However much his proceedings will have amused you, you will not remember his exact words. What you will remember is that he said that the sole was not a sole, but a blank, blank, blank plaice; that the cook ought to be shot, by God he ought to be shot. The plaice had been out of the water two years, and it had been caught in a drain: all that there was of Dieppe about this Sole Dieppoise was something that you cannot remember. You will remember this gentleman's starting eyes, his grunts between words, that he was fond of saying "damnable, damnable, damnable." You will also remember that the man at the same table with you was talking about morals, and that your boots were too tight, whilst you were trying, in your under mind, to arrange a meeting with some lady. . . .

So that, if you had to render that scene or those speeches for purposes of fiction, you would not give a word for word re-invention of sustained sentences from the gentleman who was dissatisfied; or if you were going to invent that scene, you would not so invent those speeches and set them down with all the panoply of inverted commas, notes of exclamation. No, you would give an impression of the whole thing, of the snorts, of the characteristic exclamation, of your friend's disquisition on morals, a few phrases of which you would intersperse into the monologue of the gentleman dissatisfied with his sole. And you would give a sense that your feet were burning, and that the lady you wanted to meet had very clear and candid eyes. You would give a little description of her hair. . . .

In that way you would attain to the sort of odd vibration that scenes in real life really have; you would give your reader the impression that he was witnessing something real, that he was passing through an experience. . . . You will observe also that you will have produced something that is very like a Futurist picture—not a Cubist picture, but one of those canvases that show you in one corner a pair of stays, in another a bit of of the foyer of a music hall, in another a fragment of early morning landscape, and in the middle a pair of eyes, the whole bearing the title of "A Night Out." And, indeed, those Futurists are only trying to render on canvas what Impressionists *tel que moi* have been trying to render for many years. (You may remember Emma's love scene at the cattle show in *Madame Bovary*.)

Do not, I beg you, be led away by the English reviewer's cant phrase to the effect that the Futurists are trying to be literary and the plastic arts can never be literary. Les Jeunes of to-day are trying all sorts of experiments, in all sorts of media. And they are perfectly right to be trying them.

IV

I have been trying to think what are the objections to Impressionism as I understand it—or rather what alternative method could be found. It seems to me that one is an Impressionist because one tries to produce an illusion of reality—or rather the business of Impressionism is to produce that illusion. The subject is one enormously complicated and is full of negatives. Thus the Impressionist author is sedulous to avoid letting his personality appear in the course of his book. On the other hand, his whole book, his whole poem is merely an expression of his personality. Let me illustrate exactly what I mean. You set out to write a story, or you set out to write a poem, and immediately your attempt becomes one creating an illusion. You attempt to involve the reader amongst the personages of the story or in the atmosphere of the poem. You do this by presentation and by presentation and again by presentation. The moment you depart from presentation, the moment you allow yourself, as a poet, to introduce the ejaculation:

O Muse Pindarian, aid me to my theme;

or the moment that, as a story-teller, you permit yourself the luxury of saying:

Now, gentle reader, is my heroine not a very sweet and oppressed lady?—

at that very moment your reader's illusion that he is present at an affair in real life or that he has been transported by your poem into an atmosphere entirely other than that of his arm-chair or his chimney-corner—at that very moment that illusion will depart. Now the point is this:

The other day I was discussing these matters with a young man whose avowed intention is to sweep away Impressionism.

And, after I had energetically put before him the views that I have here expressed, he simply remarked: "Why try to produce an illusion?" To which I could only reply: "Why then write?"

I have asked myself frequently since then why one should try to produce an illusion of reality in the mind of one's reader. Is it just an occupation like any other—like postage-stamp collecting, let us say—or is it the sole end and aim of art? I have spent the greater portion of my working life in preaching that particular doctrine: is it possible, then, that I have been entirely wrong?

Of course it is possible for any man to be entirely wrong; but I confess myself to being as yet unconverted. The chief argument of my futurist friend was that producing an illusion causes the writer so much trouble as not to be worth while. That does not seem to me to be an argument worth very much because—and again I must say it seems to me—the business of an artist is surely to take trouble, but this is probably doing my friend's position, if not his actual argument, an injustice. I am aware that there are quite definite æsthetic objections to the business of producing an illusion. In order to produce an illusion you must justify; in order to justify you must introduce a certain amount of matter that may not appear germane to your story or to your poem. Sometimes, that is to say, it would appear as if for the purpose of proper bringing out of a very slight Impressionist sketch the artist would need an altogether disproportionately enormous frame; a frame absolutely monstrous. Let me again illustrate exactly what I mean. It is not sufficient to say: "Mr Jones was a gentleman who had a strong aversion to rabbit-pie." It is not sufficient, that is to say, if Mr Jones's dislike for rabbit-pie is an integral part of your story. And it is quite possible that a dislike for one form or other of food might form the integral part of a story. Mr Jones might be a hard-worked coal-miner with a well-meaning wife, whom he disliked because he was developing a passion for a frivolous girl. And it might be quite possible that one evening the well-meaning wife, not knowing her husband's peculiarities, but desiring to give him a special and extra treat, should purchase from a stall a couple of rabbits and spend many hours in preparing for him a pie of great succulence, which should be a solace to him when he returns, tired with his labours and rendered nervous by his growing passion for the other lady. The rabbit-pie would then become a symbol—a symbol of the whole tragedy of life. It would symbolize for Mr Jones the whole of his wife's want of sympathy for him and the whole of his distaste for her; his reception of it would symbolize for Mrs Jones the whole hopelessness of her life, since she had expended upon it inventiveness, sedulous care, sentiment, and a good will. From that position, with the rabbit-pie always in the centre of the discussion, you might work up to the murder of Mrs Jones, to Mr Jones's elopement with the other lady—to any tragedy that you liked. For indeed the position contains, as you will perceive, the whole tragedy of life.

And the point is this, that if your tragedy is to be absolutely convincing, it is not sufficient to introduce the fact of Mr Jones's dislike for rabbit-pie by the bare statement. According to your temperament you must sufficiently account for that dislike. You might do it by giving Mr Jones a German grandmother, since all Germans have a peculiar loathing for the rabbit and regard its flesh as unclean. You might then find it necessary to account for the dislike the Germans have for these little creatures; you might have to state that his dislike is a self-preservative race instinct, since in Germany the rabbit is apt to eat certain poisonous fungi, so that one out of every ten will cause the death of its consumer, or you might proceed with your justification of Mr Jones's dislike for rabbit-pie along different lines. You might say that it was a nervous aversion caused by having been violently thrashed when a boy by his father at a time when a rabbit-pie was upon the table. You might then have to go on to justify the nervous temperament of Mr Jones by saying that his mother drank or that his father was a man too studious for his position. You might have to pursue almost endless studies in the genealogy of Mr Jones; because, of course, you might want to account for the studiousness of Mr Jones's father by making him the bastard son of a clergyman, and then you might want to account for the libidinous habits of the clergyman in question. That will be simply a matter of your artistic conscience.

You have to make Mr Jones's dislike for rabbits convincing. You have to make it in the first place convincing to your reader alone; but the odds are that you will try to make it convincing also to yourself, since you yourself in this solitary world of ours will be the only reader that you really and truly know. Now all these attempts at justification, all these details of parentage and the like, may very well prove uninteresting to your reader. They are, however, necessary if your final effect of murder is to be a convincing impression.

But again, if the final province of art is to convince, its first province is to interest. So that, to the extent that your justification is uninteresting, it is an artistic defect. It may sound paradoxical, but the truth is that your Impressionist can only get his strongest effects by using beforehand a great deal of what one may call non-Impressionism. He will make, that is to say, an enormous impression on his reader's mind by the use or three words. But very likely each one of those three words will be prepared for by ten thousand other words. Now are we to regard those other words as being entirely unnecessary, as being, that is to say, so many artistic defects? That I take to be my futurist friend's ultimate assertion.

Says he: "All these elaborate conventions of Conrad or of Maupassant give the reader the impression that a story is being told—all these meetings of bankers and master-mariners in places like the Ship Inn at Greenwich, and all Maupassant's dinner-parties, always in the politest circles, where a countess or a fashionable doctor or someone relates a passionate or a pathetic or a tragic or a merely grotesque incident—as you have it, for instance, in the 'Contes de la Bécasse'—all this machinery for getting a story told is so much waste of time. A story is a story; why not just tell it anyhow? You can never tell what sort of an impression you will produce upon a reader. Then why bother about Impressionism? Why not just chance your luck?"

There is a good deal to be said for this point of view. Writing up to my own standards is such an intolerable labour and such a thankless job, since it can't give me the one thing in the world that I desire—that for my part I am determined to drop creative writing for good and all. But I, like all writers of my generation, have been so handicapped that there is small wonder that one should be tired out. On the one hand the difficulty of getting hold of any critical guidance was, when I was a boy, insuperable. There was nothing. Criticism was non-existent; self-conscious art was decried; you were supposed to write by inspiration; you were the young generation with the vine-leaves in your hair, knocking furiously at the door. On the other hand, one writes for money, for fame, to excite the passion of love, to make an impression upon one's time. Well, God knows what one writes for. But it is certain that one gains neither fame nor money; certainly one does not excite the passion of love, and one's time continues to be singularly unimpressed.

But young writers to-day have a much better chance, on the æsthetic side at least. Here and there, in nooks and corners, they can find someone to discuss their work, not from the point of view of goodness or badness or of niceness or of nastiness, but from the simple point of view of expediency. The moment you can say: "Is it expedient to print *vers libre* in long or short lines, or in the form of prose, or not to print it at all, but to recite it?"—the moment you can find someone to discuss these expediences calmly, or the moment that you can find someone with whom to discuss the relative values of justifying your character or of abandoning the attempt to produce an illusion of reality—at that moment you are very considerably helped; whereas an admirer of your work might fall down and kiss your feet and it would not be of the very least use to you.

V

This adieu, like Herrick's, to poesy, may seem to be a digression. Indeed it is; and indeed it isn't. It is, that is to say, a digression in the sense that it is a statement not immediately germane to the argument that I am carrying on. But it is none the less an insertion fully in accord with the canons of Impressionism as I understand it. For the first business of Impressionism is to produce an impression, and the only way in literature to produce an impression is to awaken interest. And, in a sustained argument, you can only keep interest awakened by keeping alive, by whatever means you may have at your disposal, the surprise of your reader. You must state your argument; you must illustrate it, and then you must stick in something that appears to have nothing whatever to do with either subject or illustration, so that the reader will exclaim: "What the devil is the fellow driving at?" And then you must go on in the same way—arguing, illustrating and startling and arguing, startling and illustrating—until at the very end your contentions will appear like a ravelled skein. And then, in the last few lines, you will draw towards you the masterstring of that seeming confusion, and the whole pattern of the carpet, the whole design of the net-work will be apparent.

This method, you will observe, founds itself upon analysis of the human mind. For no human being likes listening to long and sustained arguments. Such listening is an effort, and no artist has the right to call for any effort from his audience. A picture should come out of its frame and seize the spectator.

Let us now consider the audience to which the artist should address himself. Theoretically a writer should be like the Protestant angel, a messenger of peace and goodwill towards all men. But, inasmuch as the Wingless Victory appears monstrously hideous to a Hottentot, and a beauty of Tunis detestable to the inhabitants of these fortunate islands, it is obvious that each artist must adopt a frame of mind, less Catholic possibly, but certainly more Papist, and address himself, like the angel of the Vulgate, only *hominibus bonæ voluntatis*. He must address himself to such men as be of goodwill; that is to say, he must typify for himself a human soul in sympathy with his own; a silent listener who will be attentive to him, and whose mind acts very much as his acts. According to the measure of this artist's identity with his species, so will be the measure of his temporal greatness. That is why a book, to be really popular, must be either extremely good or extremely bad. For Mr Hall Caine has millions of readers; but then Guy de Maupassant and Flaubert have tens of millions.

I suppose the proposition might be put in another way. Since the great majority of mankind are, on the surface, vulgar and trivial—the stuff to fill graveyards—the great majority of mankind will be easily and quickly affected by art which is vulgar and trivial. But, inasmuch as this world is a very miserable purgatory for most of us sons of men—who remain stuff with which graveyards are filled—inasmuch as horror, despair and incessant strivings are the lot of the most trivial of humanity, who endure them as a rule with commonsense and cheerfulness—so, if a really great master strike the note of horror, of despair, of striving, and so on, he will stir chords in the hearts of a larger number of people than those who are moved by the merely vulgar and the merely trivial. This is probably why *Madame Bovary* has sold more copies than any book ever published, except, of course, books purely religious. But the appeal of religious books is exactly similar.

It may be said that the appeal of *Madame Bovary* is largely sexual. So it is, but it is only in countries like England and the United States that the abominable tortures of sex—or, if you will, the abominable interests of sex—are not supposed to take rank alongside of the horrors of lost honour, commercial ruin, or death itself. For all these things are the components of life, and each is of equal importance.

So, since Flaubert is read in Russia, in Germany, in France, in the United States, amongst the non-Anglo-Saxon population, and by the immense populations of South America, he may be said to have taken for his audience the whole of the world that could possibly be expected to listen to a man of his race. (I except, of course, the Anglo-Saxons who cannot be confidently expected to listen to anything other than the words produced by Mr George Edwardes, and musical comedy in general.)

My futurist friend again visited me yesterday, and we discussed this very question of audiences. Here again he said that I was entirely wrong. He said that an artist should not address himself to *l'homme moyen sensuel*, but to intellectuals, to people who live at Hampstead and wear no hats. (He withdrew his contention later.)

I maintain on my own side that one should address oneself to the cabmen round the corner, but this also is perhaps an exaggeration. My friend's contention on behalf of the intellectuals was not so much due to his respect for their intellects. He said that they knew the A B C of an art, and that it is better to address yourself to an audience that knows the A B C of an art than to an audience entirely untrammelled by such knowledge. In this I think he was wrong, for the intellectuals are persons of very conventional mind, and they acquire as a rule simultaneously with the A B C of any art the knowledge of so many conventions that it is almost impossible to make any impression upon their minds. Hampstead and the hatless generally offer an impervious front to futurisms, simply because they have imbibed from Whistler and the Impressionists the convention that painting should not be literary. Now every futurist picture tells a story; so that rules out futurism. Similarly with the cubists. Hampstead has imbibed, from God knows where, the dogma that all art should be based on life, or should at least draw its inspiration and its strength from the representation of nature. So there goes cubism, since cubism is non-representational, has nothing to do with life, and has a quite proper contempt of nature.

When I produced my argument that one should address oneself to the cabmen at the corner, my futurist friend at once flung to me the jeer about Tolstoi and the peasant. Now the one sensible thing in the long drivel of nonsense with which Tolstoi misled this dull world was the remark that art should be addressed to the peasant. My futurist friend said that that was sensible for an artist living in Russia or Roumania, but it was an absurd remark to be let fall by a critic living on Campden Hill. His view was that you cannot address yourself to the peasant unless that peasant have evoked folk-song or folk-lores. I don't know why that was his view, but that was his view.

It seems to me to be nonsensical, even if the inner meaning of his dictum was that art should be addressed to a community of practising artists. Art, in fact, should be addressed to those who are not preoccupied. It is senseless to address a Sirventes to a man who is going mad with love, and an Imagiste poem will produce little effect upon another man who is going through the bankruptcy court.

It is probable that Tolstoi thought that in Russia the non-preoccupied mind was to be found solely amongst the peasant class, and that is why he said that works of art should be addressed to the peasant. I don't know how it may be in Russia, but certainly in Occidental Europe the non-preoccupied mind—which is the same thing as the peasant intelligence—is to be found scattered throughout every grade of society. When I used just now the instances of a man mad for love, or distracted by the prospect of personal ruin, I was purposely misleading. For a man mad as a hatter for love of a worthless creature, or a man maddened by the tortures of bankruptcy, by dishonour or by failure, may yet have, by the sheer necessity of his nature, a mind more receptive than most other minds. The mere craving for relief from his personal thoughts may make him take quite unusual interest in a work of art. So that is not preoccupation in my intended sense, but for a moment the false statement crystallised quite clearly what I was aiming at.

The really impassible mind is not the mind quickened by passion, but the mind rendered slothful by preoccupation purely trivial. The "English gentleman" is, for instance, an absolutely hopeless being from this point of view. His mind is so taken up by considerations of what is good form, of what is good feeling, of what is even good fellowship; he is so concerned to pass unnoticed in the crowd; he is so set upon having his room like everyone else's room, that he will find it impossible to listen to any plea for art which is exceptional, vivid, or startling. The cabman, on the other hand, does not mind being thought a vulgar sort of bloke; in consequence he will form a more possible sort of audience. On the other hand, amongst the purely idler classes it is perfectly possible to find individuals who are so firmly and titularly gentle folk that they don't have to care a damn what they do. These again are possible audiences for the artist. The point is really, I take it, that the preoccupation that is fatal to art is the moral or the social preoccupation. Actual preoccupations matter very little. Your cabman may drive his taxi through exceedingly difficult streets; he may have half-a-dozen close shaves in a quarter of an hour. But when those things are over they are over, and he has not the necessity of a cabman. His point of view as to what is art, good form, or, let us say, the proper relation of the sexes, is unaffected. He may be a hungry man, a thirsty man, or even a tired man, but he will not necessarily have his finger upon his moral pulse, and he will not hold as æsthetic dogma the idea that no painting must tell a story, or the moral dogma that passion only becomes respectable when you have killed it.

It is these accursed dicta that render an audience hopeless to the artist, that render art a useless pursuit and the artist himself a despised individual.

So that those are the best individuals for an artist's audience who have least listened to accepted ideas—who are acquainted with deaths at street corners, with the marital infidelities of crowded courts, with the goodness of heart of the criminal, with the meanness of the undetected or the sinless, who know the queer odd jumble of negatives that forms our miserable and hopeless life. If I had to choose as reader I would rather have one who had never read anything before but the Newgate Calendar, or the records of crime, starvation and divorce in the Sunday paper—I would rather have him for a reader than a man who had discovered the song that the sirens sang, or had by heart the whole of the *Times Literary Supplement,* from its inception to the present day. Such a peasant intelligence will know that this is such a queer world that anything may be possible. And that is the type of intelligence that we need.

Of course, it is more difficult to find these intelligences in the town than in the rural districts. A man thatching all day long has time for many queer thoughts; so has a man who from sunrise to sunset is trimming a hedge into shape with a bagging hook. I have, I suppose, myself thought more queer thoughts when digging potatoes than at any other time during my existence. It is, for instance, very queer if you are digging potatoes in the late evening, when it has grown cool after a very hot day, to thrust your hand into the earth after a potato and to find that the earth is quite warm—is about flesh-heat. Of course, the clods would be warm because the sun would have been shining on them all day, and the air gives up its heat much quicker than the earth. But it is none the less a queer sensation.

Now, if the person experiencing that sensation have what I call a peasant intelligence, he will just say that it is a queer thing and will store it away in his mind along with his other experiences. It will go along with the remembrance of hard frost, of fantastic icicles, the death of rabbits pursued by stoats, the singularly quick ripening of corn in a certain year, the fact that such and such a man was overlooked by a wise woman and so died because, his wife, being tired of him, had paid the wise woman five sixpences which she had laid upon the table in the form of a crown; or along with the other fact that a certain man murdered his wife by the use of a packet of sheep dip which he had stolen from a field where the farmer was employed at lamb washing. All these remembrances he will have in his mind, not classified under any headings of social reformers, or generalized so as to fulfil any fancied moral law.

But the really dangerous person for the artist will be the gentleman who, chancing to put his hand into the ground and to find it about as warm as the breast of a woman, if you could thrust your hand between her chest and her stays, will not accept the experience as an experience, but will start talking about the breast of mother-nature. This last man is the man whom the artist should avoid, since he will regard phenomena not as phenomena, but as happenings, with which he may back up preconceived dogmas—as, in fact, so many sticks with which to beat a dog.

No, what the artist needs is the man with the quite virgin mind—the man who will not insist that grass must always be painted green, because all the poets, from Chaucer till the present day, had insisted on talking about the green grass, or the green leaves, or the green straw.

Such a man, if he comes to your picture and sees you have painted a haycock bright purple will say:

"Well, I have never myself observed a haycock to be purple, but I can understand that if the sky is very blue and the sun is setting very red, the shady side of the haycock might well appear to be purple." That is the kind of peasant intelligence that the artist needs for his audience.

And the whole of Impressionism comes to this: having realized that the audience to which you will address yourself must have this particular peasant intelligence, or, if you prefer it, this particular and virgin openness of mind, you will then figure to yourself an individual, a silent listener, who shall be to yourself the *homo bonæ voluntatis*—man of goodwill. To him, then, you will address your picture, your poem, your prose story, or your argument. You will seek to capture his interest; you will seek to hold his interest. You will do this by methods of surprise, of fatigue, by passages of sweetness in your language, by passages suggesting the sudden and brutal shock of suicide. You will give him passages of dulness, so that your bright effects may seem more bright; you will alternate, you will dwell for a long time upon an intimate point; you will seek to exasperate so that you may the better enchant. You will, in short, employ all the devices of the prostitute. If you are too proud for this you may be the better gentleman or the better lady, but you will be the worse artist. For the artist must always be humble and humble and again humble, since before the greatness of his task he himself is nothing. He must again be outrageous, since the greatness of his task calls for enormous excesses by means of which he may recoup his energies. That is why the artist is, quite rightly, regarded with suspicion by people who desire to live in tranquil and ordered society.

But one point is very important. The artist can never write to satisfy himself—to get, as the saying is, something off the chest. He must not write propaganda which it is his desire to write; he must not write rolling periods, the production of which gives him a soothing feeling in his digestive organs or wherever it is. He must write always so as to satisfy that other fellow—that other fellow who has too clear an intelligence to let his attention be captured or his mind deceived by special pleadings in favour of any given dogma. You must not write so as to improve him, since he is a much better fellow than yourself, and you must not write so as to influence him, since he is a granite rock, a peasant intelligence, the gnarled bole of a sempiternal oak, against which you will dash yourself in vain. It is in short no pleasant kind of job to be a conscious artist. You won't have any vine-leaves in your poor old hair; you won't just dash your quill into an inexhaustible ink-well and pour out fine frenzies. No, you will be just the skilled workman doing his job with drill or chisel or mallet. And you will get precious little out of it. Only, just at times, when you come to look again at some work of yours that you have quite forgotten, you will say, "Why, that is rather well done." That is all.

Ford Madox Hueffer, "On Impressionism," *Poetry and Drama*, II (June, December 1914), 161–175, 323–334.

Techniques

Ford's fascination with the process of artistic creation never deserted him, and until his death in 1939, he was continually reconsidering the problem of technique. In reviews and articles like the one printed below, he published his views as they changed and developed. All of his life he was essentially an Impressionist, but he was never entirely satisfied with his methods, realizing always the need for compromise. Thus in 1924, for example, when he sent a complimentary copy of Some Do Not *to Conrad, he observed: "You'll notice I've abandoned attempts at indirect reporting of speech—as an experiment. How late in life does one go on experimenting?" By the mid-thirties he was still trying new techniques, and talking about them, but for illustrative material he generally used the work of others. In this way, he was able to combine critical appreciation with his own experimentation.*

"Techniques" originally appeared in The Southern Review *which was founded by Robert Penn Warren and a group of Southern writers in 1935. Ford went to Louisiana to take part in a symposium devoted to the literature of the South and as a famous editor who had presided over a number of literary movements, he delivered the principal address and appeared in the first number of the new review.*

I

Technique is perhaps the most odious word in the English language. I hope that by adding the above "s" some of the odium may be dispelled. It is necessary from time to time to emphasize the fact that writing in general and imaginative writing in particular are the products of craftsmanship. In the middle ages a craft was called a mystery. It is a good word, for it is a mystery why we write and a mystery how great writers do it.

They do it by observing certain rules—or after having observed certain rules for a long time, by jumping off from them. You may if you like say that great literatures have only arisen when technical rules have been jumped off from—Shakespeare and the Elizabethans having jumped off from the classicisms of *Ferrex and Porrex;* the Cockney School of Poetry from the classical stultifications of an Eighteenth Century in decay; or Flaubert and the French, English, and American Impressionists, whose methods I propose here to analyse for you, from the classical slipshodnesses that preceded them. The case of the Impressionists differs from that of the others, however, in that they practised, and, when they had the time, enjoined, a tightening rather than any slackening of the rules.

Sang Mr. Kipling:

> There are five and forty ways
> Of inditing tribal lays
> And every single one of them is right!

That is to say that Mr. Kipling, having proved himself an extraordinarily great master of the most difficult of all crafts— that of the short and short-long story writer—had to hasten to excuse himself by proving that at heart he was, and always meant to be, an English gentleman. For the English gentleman may write . . . but before all things he must not be a writer. He may, that is to say, at odd moments sit down and toss off something, but he must not do it earnestly or according to any rules. Or, if he does observe any rules, he must hasten, hasten, hasten to assert that he does not. Otherwise he would not be received in really good drawing-rooms.

I do not mean to assert that occasionally a masterpiece may not be tossed off or that the roll of Royal and Noble Authors does not number a master or two. You have Clarendon who wrote the *History of the Rebellion,* Beckford who wrote the *Letters from Portugal* . . . But how much more Clarendon might we not have had, had he not been father to a queen, or how much more

Beckford, had he not found it necessary to be the nabob-builder of Fonthill? And above all, how much more Cunninghame Graham if Mr. Robert Bontine Cunninghame Graham had not happened to be, in addition to the 'incomparable writer of English,' Earl of Monteith, King of Scotland if he had his rights, and the very spit and image of his connection, Henri IV of France.

That indeed is the real tragedy of English literature . . . is why England has in fact no literature but only some great, isolated peaks. For, to possess a Literature, a country must have a whole cloud—or better still, a whole populace—of writers instinct with a certain skill in, a certain respect for, a certain productivity of, writing. You must in that country be able to go, say to a railway bookstall, and by merely stretching out a random hand, take the first book that comes and find it to be, for certain, well written, well constructed, instinct with a certain knowledge of the values of life—such a work in short, as a proper man may let himself be seen reading without loss of self-respect. You can do that in France, you could do it in Germany before Mr. Hitler began his burnings; you are beginning to be able to do it in the United States. But in the home and cradle of the writings of our race you have not been able to do it since the XVIIth Century—when of course there were no railway bookstalls. It is only a respect for a technique that can ensure this form of civilization for a country because the writing of books is a difficult matter—the writing of any kind of book.

I am going to write particularly about the writing of works of the imagination—and specifically about the writing of novels. But the factual book is susceptible of, and gains as much by, care in construction, and the poem gains as much by attention to lucidity or verbiage and progression of effect, as does any novel. The convention of the narrative is as important to the historian of the battle of Minden as it is to the novelist trembling lest any slip in his construction should make his reader slacken or altogether lose his interest.

And the real difference between the writers of the Impressionist group, who since the days of Flaubert have dominated the public mind, and their predecessors is that the post-Flaubertians have studied, primarily, to hold just that public mind, whilst their predecessors, though wishing obviously to be read, never gave a thought to how interest may be inevitably—and almost scientifically—aroused. The novelist from, say, Richardson to Meredith thought that he had done his job when he had set down a simple tale beginning with the birth of his hero or his heroine and ending when the ring of marriage bells completed the simple convention. But the curious thing was that he never gave a thought to how stories are actually told or even to how the biographies of one's friends come gradually before one.

The main difference between a novel by the forgotten James Payne—who in his day was a much respected and not too popular novelist—and a work of the unforgettable author of *The Turn of the Screw,* who also, you will observe was a much respected and certainly not too popular novelist, is that the one recounts whilst the other presents. The one makes statements; the other builds suggestions of happenings on suggestions of happenings.

On the face of it you would say that the way to tell a story is to begin at the beginning and go soberly through to the end, making here and there a reflection that shall show that you, the author who is to be forever present in the reader's mind, are a person of orthodox morals and what the French call *bien pensant.*

But already by the age of Flaubert, the novelist had become uneasily aware that if the author is perpetually, with his reflections, distracting his reader's attention from the story, the story must lose interest. Some one noticed that in *Vanity Fair* when Mr. Thackeray had gradually built up a state of breathless interest and Becky Sharp on the eve of Waterloo had seemed almost audibly to breathe and palpitate before your eyes, suddenly the whole illusion went to pieces. You were back in your study before the fire reading a book of made-up stuff though the moment before, you would have sworn you were in Brussels amongst the revellers ... And that disillusionment was occasioned by Mr. Thackeray, broken nose and all, thrusting his moral reflections upon you, in the desperate determination to impress you with the conviction that he was a proper man to be a member of the *Athenaeum Club* ... He had, with immense but untrained and unreflecting genius, built up a whole phantasmagoria of realities in which his reader really felt himself walking amongst the actors in the real life of the desperate day that preceded Waterloo ... And then the whole illusion went.

It would be idle to say that it was Flaubert who first observed that the intrusion of the author destroyed the illusion of the reader. Such ideas arise sporadically across the literary landscape and get finally adopted by one or other of the distinguished though, long before that, they will have been in the air. And Flaubert more than any of his associates clamored unceasingly and passionately that the author must be impersonal, must, like a creating deity, stand neither for nor against any of his characters, must project and never report and must, above all, forever keep himself out of his books. He must write his books as if he were rendering the impressions of a person present at a scene; he must remember that a person present at a scene does not see everything and is above all not able to remember immensely long passages of dialogue.

These dicta were unceasingly discussed by the members of Flaubert's set who included the Goncourts, Turgenev, Gautier, Maupassant and, in a lesser degree, Zola and the young James— this last as disciple of the gentle Russian genius. They met in different cafés and restaurants from the Café Procope which still exists, if fallen from its high estate, to Brébant's which has now disappeared. And their discussions were frenetic and violent. They discussed the *minutiae* of words and their economical employment; the *charpente,* the architecture, of the novel; the handling of dialogue; the renderings of impressions; the impersonality of the author. They discussed these things with the passion of politicians inciting to rebellion. And in those *coenaculae* the modern novel—the immensely powerful engine of our civilization—was born.

You get an admirable idea of the violence of these discussions from the several accounts that exist of the desperate encounter that took place between the young James and the giant of Croisset over a point of the style of Merimée. The assembly, it would seem, had been almost unanimous in its contempt for the style

of Merimée and the young James, sitting, a *jeune homme modeste,*
as he afterwards used to style me, in the shadow of Turgenev, had
ventured to join in the chorus. But that an American should dare
to open his mouth in those discussions proved too much for the
equanimity of Flaubert. He said so. He said with violence ... To
think that an American should dare to have views as to the
French of one of the greatest of France's stylists! Only to think it,
was enough to make Villon, Ronsard, Racine, Corneille, Chateaubriand—not of course that their styles were anything to write
home about—turn in their graves ...

The pale young James was, it is recorded, led away by the
beautiful Russian genius who, nevertheless, induced that brave
young trans-Atlantic to call with him next day upon the giant
who had inflicted that flagellation. And Flaubert, as I have elsewhere recorded, received Turgenev and his young American
friend in his dressing-gown, opening his front door himself, a
thing that, till the end of his life, Mr. James regarded as supremely shocking.

I don't mind repeating myself in the effort to emphasize how
absolutely international a thing literature is. For Henry James,
retiring to an England that appeared to him to be all one large
deer park across which the sunlight fell upon ubiquitous haunts
of ancient peace—the young James then, like those birds who,
carrying the viscous seeds of the mistletoe on their bills and claws,
establish always new colonies of the plant of the Druids, planted
for a little while in the country of my birth the seeds of the novel
as it at present exists.

It is said that James directly influenced Conrad in his incessant search for a new form for the novel. Nothing could be more
literally false but nothing could be more impressionistically true.
London was at that date—the earlier nineties—a veritable bacteri-
ologist's soup for the culture of modern germs, and the author of
Daisy Miller, Roderick Hudson, and *The Princess Casamassima,*
being enthusiastically received in a city that was weary to death
of the novels of James Payne, William Black, and the rest of the
more or less respected, sowed around him, like the mistletoe-
spreading birds, an infinite number of literary Impressionist

germs. And if Conrad, as is literally true, learned nothing directly of James, yet he found prepared for him a medium in which, slowly at first but with an always increasing impetus, his works could spread. It was the London of the *Yellow Book,* of R. L. Stevenson, that sedulous ape, of W. E. Henley, that harsh-mouthed but very beneficent spreader of French influences.

It was a city of infinite curiosity as to new literary methods and of an infinite readiness to assimilate new ideas, whether they came from Paris by way of Ernest Dowson, from Poland by way of Conrad, or from New York or New England by way of Henry James, Stephen Crane, Harold Frederick, or Whistler, Abbey, Sargent, and George Boughton. London had in fact been visited by one of its transitory phases in which nothing seemed good but what came from abroad. We were to see another such phase in '13 and '14 in the flowering days of Ezra Pound, John Gould Fletcher, Robert Frost, Marinetti, the Cubists, the Vorticists, and how many other foreign movements that were to be crushed in the bud by the iron shards of war. We may see another tomorrow. At any rate it is overdue. * * *

II

I began by writing the word 'techniques' rather than 'technique,' so as to soften the impact on the ear of that harsh dissyllable. For there is not one only Technique, a chill enemy of mankind known only to and arbitrarily prescribed by a pedantic circle of the highbrow *intelligentsia*. Not one only, but just as many as there are writers, each one differing by a shade, the one from the other, until the difference between the leader of the advancing line and the boy at its end is as great as that that lies between the limpidities of Merimée and the clouds of virtuosities of *Du Côté de Chez Swann* or of *Ulysses*. Yet we are all going to Heaven and Turgenev shall be of the company.

Mr. Kipling was perfectly right when he wrote that there are five and forty ways for the writer. There are probably five hundred thousand, every single one of them being right. But to tell the whole truth, he must have added that there is only one best way for the treatment of every given subject and only one method best suited for every given writer. And such advocates of the study of technique as Conrad or Dowson or James or Crane or Flaubert are far more interested in the writer's finding himself than in establishing any one rule that shall cover every tribal lay. The young writer, for whom I am principally writing, or the old man setting up as writer, will inevitably—and very properly—go through the stage of expressing himself. He will inevitably desire to get out of his system his reactions to sex, wine, music, homosexuality, parents, puritanism, death, life, immortality, technocracy, communism and existence amongst the infinite flatnesses beneath the suns and tornadoes of the Middle West or the Mississippi Delta. But once all that *Sturm und Drang*—once that milk fever—is inscribed on fair paper, the joys of autobiography are past. The aspirant finds himself faced, if he is to continue writer, with the drear necessity of rendering one human affair or another. It is then that he will have to go in search of a technique that will suit him as well as the one fishing-cane that will be indispensable to him if he is to cast his fly exactly upstream before the jaws of the waiting trout. For there are innumerable techniques but only one best one for each writer.

What then is a technique? It is a device by which a writer may appeal to his fellows—to so many of his fellows that, in the end, he may claim to have appealed to all humanity from China to the Tierra del Fuego. Nothing less will satisfy the ardent writer —the really ardent and agonisingly passionate renderer of affairs like Flaubert or James. And there are some who attain to that stupendous reward. At any rate I have been informed by a German firm of world-book distributors that the one book that they export all over the world—to Rio de Janeiro as to the Straits Settlements, to Prague as to Berkeley, Cal., and Pekin is—*Madame Bovary*.

This does not mean that I am asking the neophyte to pass his life writing *pastiches* of the affair in which poor Emma was involved. But it does mean that, if he is a prudent man, he will read that book and *Education Sentimentale* and *Bouvard et Pecuchet* a great many times, over and over again, with minute scrutiny, to discover what in Flaubert's methods is eternal and universal in appeal. And having discovered what he thinks that to be, he must experiment for a long time to see whether he can work in that method as easily as he can live in an old and utterly comfortable coat ... or dressing gown. And so he must go on to other writers. For the history of Emma Bovary is not alone amongst world-and-all-time best sellers. Next to that, and circling the globe in flights almost as numerous, come the *Pilgrim's Progress* and the *Pickwick Papers* ... And long before them stands the *Imitation of Christ* and a little after that the *Holy Bible*. To each of these works, not excluding the religious masterpieces, the neophyte may well apply his microscopes and his diminishing glasses. At the last he shall come into his own.

He will come into his own when, reading those works a final time in a spirit of forgetfulness, for pleasure and with critical faculties put to sleep, he shall say: "Such and such a passage pleases me," and casting back into his subconsciousness shall add: "This fellow gets that effect by a cadenced paragraph of long, complicated sentences, interspersed with shorter statements, ending with a long, dying fall of words and the final taptaptap of a three monosyllabled phrase ..." Just like that.

That was the quite conscious practice of Conrad when seeking to be dramatic as it was the only less conscious practice of Flaubert. And, if you will read again my last paragraph, you will see how dramatic—how even a thought vulgar—such a cadence may be.

Or it may be that the devices of Conrad and Flaubert, as you take them to be, do not suit your book after your painful studies. Or you may say that Flaubert in France and Conrad in America lying under temporary clouds of oblivion, you will never attain to the enviable gift of extended popularity if you let them in the slightest degree exercise an influence on you. Try then Hudson.

Hudson, or his Latin-American running mate, Mr. Cunninghame Graham, the most exquisite living of *prosateurs* in English, though of right King of Scotland. Or *The Third Violet* of Stephen Crane who for his own purposes professed to have been born and bred in the Bowery but was actually the son of some one of episcopal standing. You will discover that Hudson gets his effects by an almost infinite and meticulous toning down of language. If you should be fortunate enough to get hold of some of his proofsheets, you will see that he simplifies to the utmost and then beyond. I remember observing—for I went once or twice through his proofs for him—that he had once written: "The buds developed into leaves." He substituted "grew," for "developed." And, finally the passage ran: "They became leaves" ... But of course, behind Huddie's prose there was that infinitely patient temperament of the naturalist, that infinite conscientiousness of observation, that have given the world White's *Natural History of Selborne*, the few writings of Thomas Edward, the Scottish naturalist—who taught *me* all I know of cadences; as well as the *Sportsman's Sketches* of Turgenev with its matchless *Bielshin Prairie* and, only yesterday, Miss Gordon's *Aleck Maury*, which has a singular spiritual kinship to the *Recits d'un Chasseur*. But that quality is the product of a temperament. You may have it or you may not. If you have it you will write beautifully—but you can never acquire it. The longest study of Hudson or Turgenev will do no more for you than turn you into a writer of *pastiches*. Galsworthy would have been a real major writer if Mr. Edward Garnett had not forced him to read Mrs. Garnett's wonderful translation of *Fathers and Children*.

But by all means read them for the exquisite pleasure they will give you.

Mr. Graham you may read as self-consciously as you will. His prose is always aristocratically unbuttoned; he approaches his subjects with the contemptuous negligence of the Highland Scottish noble or the Southern plantation owner. But that very contempt gives him a power of keying down drama till the result is an economy or resource such as only Stephen Crane, himself aristocratically contemptuous, has otherwise attained. There is a short—a very short—story of Mr. Graham's called "Beattock for Moffatt"—the railway porter's cry meaning: 'Beattock, change for Moffatt'—which is one of the great tragedies. It projects nothing more than the railway journey of a dying, homesick Scot of no importance, going home, with a vulgar and uncomprehending but not unkindly Cockney wife, to die of tuberculosis in Moffatt. His whole mind is given to seeing Moffatt again after a long obscuration in London . . . And in the keen air after the stuffy railway carriage on Beattock platform he dies, being fated never again to see Moffatt, that Carcassonne of the North . . . dies whilst the porters are still calling 'Beattock for Moffatt' . . . It is told almost as summarily as I have told it . . . but with just those differences of touch that make the passing of that obscure Scot as lamentable—nay, more lamentable!, than the death of Hector.

The secret of poor Steevie is very much akin to that of Mr. Graham, be his method of approach to his subject never so different. Mr. Graham—the Don Roberto of a hundred drawing-rooms —with contemptuous negligence does not record; Crane with nervous meticulousness excises and excises. Both having an unerring sense of the essential, the temperamental results arrived at are extraordinarily similar. A Crane drama will end:

The Girl said:

"You say . . ."

He answered:

"Observe that I have never ventured to say . . ."

She threw the third violet at his feet . . .

Something like that—for I have no copy of *The Third Violet* from which to quote—but you can observe that, a situation of poignance having been established, such an end may be of an extreme drama.

If you compare it with the famous last sentence of *The Turn of the Screw*, you will see how two writers of the same school and training, using very similar methods in all the essentials of rendering an affair, may give an entirely different temperamental turn to their endings.

"We were alone with the quiet day," wrote Mr. James confidently and beautifully, "and his little heart . . ." he continues confidently still. But then you hear him mutter to himself. "This is too direct. This will give the effect of the *coup de canon* at the end of a Maupassant story . . . We must delay . . . We must give the effect of lingering . . . We must let the reader down gently." . . . And into the direct statement that was to be completed he inserts the qualificative word "dispossessed." "We were alone with the quiet day and his little heart had stopped," would have been reporting of a high order. But: "We were alone with the quiet day and his little heart, dispossessed, had stopped," is the supreme poetry of a great genius. And yet of an amazing economy.

But it was perhaps Crane of all that school or gang—and not excepting Maupassant—who most observed that canon of Impressionism: "You must render: never report." You must never, that is to say, write: "He saw a man aim a gat at him"; you must put it: "He saw a steel ring directed at him." Later you must get in that, in his subconsciousness, he recognized that the steel ring was the polished muzzle of a revolver. So Crane rendered it in *Three White Mice* which is one of the major short stories of the world. That is Impressionism!

III

But the great truth that must never be forgotten by you, by me, or by the neophyte at the gate, is that the purpose of a technique is to help the writer to please, and that neither writing nor the technique behind it has any other purpose. In evolving the technique that shall fit your fishing-pole you have to think of nothing but how to please your reader. By pleasing him, you hold his attention, and once you have accomplished that, you may inject into him what you please: for you need not forget, when you write a novel, the gravity of your role as educator: only you must remember that in vain does the fowler set his net in the sight of the bird. The reader wants to be filled with the feeling that you are a clever magician; he never wants to have you intruding and remarking what a good man you are.

I will try to inculcate this most important of all lessons by presenting some instances from the writers best known to myself. With all the others I have mentioned—with the exception of Flaubert who was dead, and of Maupassant who had retired from active life before I entered the bull-ring that is the literary life—with all the others I discussed literary problems and their personal techniques, debating rather strenuously with Crane and

Hudson and listening with deference to Henry James, Henry Harland, Henley, Miss Ethel Mayne, and others of the *Yellow Book* and the English-American Impressionist group.

With Conrad I descended into the arena and beside him wrestled, rain or shine, through the greater part of a decade. I will therefore now take two or three instances of details of technique and show how we approached them. Conrad, I may say, was more interested in finding a new form for the novel; I, in training myself to write *just* words that would not stick out of a sentence and so distract the reader's attention by their very justness. But we worked ceaselessly, together, on those problems, turning from the problem of the new form to that of the just word as soon as we were mentally exhausted by the one or the other.

That we did succeed eventually in finding *a* new form I think I may permit myself to claim, Conrad first evolving the convention of a Marlow who should narrate, in presentation, the whole story of a novel just as, without much sequence or pursued chronology, a story will come up into the mind of a narrator, and I eventually dispensing with a narrator but making the story come up in the mind of the unseen author with a similar want of chronological sequence. I must apologize for referring to my own work but, if I did not, this story would become rather incomprehensible and would lack an end, since after Conrad's death I pursued those investigations with a never-ceasing industry and belief in the usefulness of my task—if not to myself, then at least to others. For it is almost as useful to set up an awful example that can be avoided as to erect signposts along a road that should be taken.

We evolved then a convention for the novel and one that I think still stands. The novel must be put into the mouth of a narrator—who must be limited by probability as to what he can know of the affair that he is adumbrating. Or it must be left to the official Author and he, being almost omnipotent, may, so long as he limits himself to presenting without comment or moralization, allow himself to be considered to know almost everything that there is to know. The narration is thus a little more limited in possibilities; the 'author's book' is a little more difficult to handle.

A narrator, that is to say, being already a fictional character, may indulge in any prejudices or wrong-headednesses and any likings or dislikes for the other characters of the book, for he is just a living being like anybody else. But an author-creator, presenting his narration without passion, may not indulge in the expression of any prejudices or like any one of his characters more than any other; for, if he displays either of those weaknesses, he will to that extent weaken the illusion that he has attempted to build up. Marlow, the narrator of *Lord Jim*, may idolize his hero or anathematize his villains with the sole result that we say: "How real Marlow is!' Conrad, however, in *Nostromo* must not let any word or preference for Nostromo or Mrs. Gould or the daughters of the Garibaldino pierce through the surface of his novel or at once we should say: "Here is this tiresome person intruding again," and at once lose the thread of the tale.

You perceive, I trust, how our eyes were forever on the reader —and if, during our fifteenth perusal of *Madame Bovary* we discerned that—as Flaubert himself somewhere confesses—the sage of Croisset was actually in love with poor Emma Bovary, his creation, we hastened to observe the one to the other that *we* must never let ourselves indulge in such mental-carnal weaknesses. A giant like Flaubert might get away with it: but we must avoid temptations... So you perceive how constantly we considered the interests of You, my Lord, in case You should one day want to glance, for diversion, through the pages we were evolving.

We were, in short, producers who thought forever of the consumer. If Conrad laid it down as a law that, in introducing a character, we must always, after a few vivid words of personal description, apportion to him a speech that *must* be a characteristic generalization, it was because we were thinking of You. We knew that if we said: "Mr. X was a foul-mouthed reactionary," you would know very little about him. But if his first words, after his introduction were: "God damn it, put all filthy Liberals up against a wall, say I, and shoot out their beastly livers..." that gentleman will make on you an impression that many following pages shall scarcely efface. Whomever else you may not quite grasp, you won't forget *him*—because that is the way people present themselves in real life. You may converse with a lady for ten minutes about the fineness of the day or the number of lumps of sugar you like in your tea and you will know little about her; but let her hazard any personal and general opinion as to the major topics of life and at once you will have her labeled, docketed and put away on the collector's shelf of your curious mind.

Similarly, in evolving a technique for the presenting of conversation, I—and in this it was rather I than Conrad, just as in the evolution of the New Form it was rather Conrad than I, though each countersigned the opinion of the other and thenceforth adopted the device so evolved—I then considered for a long time how conversations presented themselves to the mind. I would find myself in a room with a gentleman who pursued an almost uninterrupted monologue. A week after, I would find that of it I retained, verbally, only his more characteristic expletives—his 'God bless my soul's,' or his 'You don't mean to say so's' and one or two short direct speeches: "If the Government goes to the country, I will bet a hundredweight of China tea to a Maltese orange that they will have a fifty-eight to forty-two majority of the voters against them." But I remembered the whole gist of his remarks.

And so, considering that an author-narrator, being supposed to have about the mnemonic powers of a man with a fair memory, will after the elapse of a certain period, be supposed to retain about that much of a conversation that the Reader may suppose him to have heard, I shall, when inventing conversations, give about just that proportion of direct and indirect speech, in which latter I shall present the gist of my character's argument . . . For, if I give more direct speech than that, the reader will say: "Confound it, how does this plaguy fellow remember an oration like that, word for word? It's impossible. So I don't believe a word he says about anything else," and he will pitch my book into the wastepaper basket . . . Of course I shall lard the indirect speeches with plenty of 'God bless my soul's' and 'Mr. X paused for a moment before continuing,' just to keep my character all the while well in the picture . . .

These of course are only two of the technical *trouvailles* that we made in labors that cannot have been exceeded by any two slaves that worked for ten years on the building of the Tower of Babel. We made an infinite number of others, covering an infinite field of human activities and reflections. You may find them valid as representing how life comes back to you and in that case they may help you, as writer, a little way along the long road that winds up hill all the way . . . All the way! For, so long as you remain a live writer, you will forever be questioning and re-questioning and testing and re-testing the devices that you will have evolved. Or they may not at all fill your bill: in which case you must go forward alone and may a gentle breeze forever temper for you the ardor of the sun's rays!

But you must—there is no other method—pursue your investigation in that spirit of ours. You must have your eyes forever on your Reader. That alone constitutes . . . Technique!

Ford Madox Ford, "Techniques," *The Southern Review*, I (July 1935), 20–25, 27–35.

Joseph Conrad

Upon Conrad's death in 1924, Ford wrote Joseph Conrad: A
Personal Remembrance, *partly as a means of paying tribute to
his former collaborator and partly to recreate the atmosphere of
their many years' work together. In the course of this book, he
paused to consider in detail the actual process of writing* The
Inheritors *and* Romance. *In doing so, he dealt specifically with
some of the technical problems alluded to above in "On Impressionism" and "Techniques." Portions from this section of* A
Personal Remembrance *are printed below.*

*This discussion is probably unique in English letters as a revelation of the actual process of literary creation. It is like entering
the novelist's study to watch him working out his methods. It is
no wonder, then, that where this book was understood, it was
appreciated. As Sinclair Lewis said of it, it "was the one great
book on the technique of writing a novel that I have ever read."*

GENERAL EFFECT

We agreed that the general effect of a novel must be the general effect that life makes on mankind. A novel must therefore
not be a narration, a report. Life does not say to you: In 1914
my next door neighbour, Mr. Slack, erected a greenhouse and
painted it with Cox's green aluminium paint. . . . If you think
about the matter you will remember, in various unordered pictures, how one day Mr. Slack appeared in his garden and contemplated the wall of his house. You will then try to remember
the year of that occurrence and you will fix it as August 1914
because having had the foresight to bear the municipal stock of
the city of Liège you were able to afford a first-class season ticket
for the first time in your life. You will remember Mr. Slack—

then much thinner because it was before he found out where to buy that cheap Burgundy of which he has since drunk an inordinate quantity though whisky you think would be much better for him! Mr. Slack again came into his garden, this time with a pale, weaselly-faced fellow, who touched his cap from time to time. Mr. Slack will point to his housewall several times at different points, the weaselly fellow touching his cap at each pointing. Some days after, coming back from business you will have observed against Mr. Slack's wall.... At this point you will remember that you were then the manager of the fresh-fish branch of Messrs. Catlin and Clovis in Fenchurch Street.... What a change since then! Millicent had not yet put her hair up.... You will remember how Millicent's hair looked, rather pale and burnished in plaits. You will remember how it now looks, henna'd: and you will see in one corner of your mind's eye a little picture of Mr. Mills the vicar talking—oh, very kindly—to Millicent after she has come back from Brighton.... But perhaps you had better not risk that. You remember some of the things said by means of which Millicent has made you cringe—and her expression!... Cox's Aluminium Paint!... You remember the half empty tin that Mr. Slack showed you—he had a most undignified cold—with the name in a horse-shoe over a blue circle that contained a red lion asleep in front of a real-gold sun....

And, if that is how the building of your neighbour's greenhouse comes back to you, just imagine how it will be with your love-affairs that are so much more complicated....

IMPRESSIONISM

We accepted without much protest the stigma: "Impressionists" that was thrown at us. In those days Impressionists were still considered to be bad people: Atheists, Reds, wearing red ties with which to frighten householders. But we accepted the name because Life appearing to us much as the building of Mr. Slack's greenhouse comes back to you, we saw that Life did not narrate, but made impressions on our brains. We in turn, if we wished to produce on you an effect of life, must not narrate but render ... impressions.

SELECTION

We agreed that the whole of Art consists in selection. To render your remembrance of your career as a fish-salesman might enhance the story of Mr. Slack's greenhouse, or it might *not*. A little image of iridiscent, blue-striped, black-striped, white fish on a white marble slab with water trickling down to them round a huge mass of orange salmon-roe; a vivid description of a horrible smell caused by a cat having stolen and hidden in the thick of your pelargoniums a cod's head that you had brought back as a perquisite, you having subsequently killed the cat with a hammer, but long, long before you had rediscovered her fishy booty. ... Such little impressions might be useful as contributing to illustrate your character—one should not kill a cat with a hammer! They might illustrate your sense of the beautiful—or your fortitude under affliction—or the diasgreeableness of Mr. Slack, who had a delicate sense of smell—or the point of view of your only daughter Millicent.

We should then have to consider whether your sense of the beautiful or your fortitude could in our rendering carry the story forward or interest the reader. If it did we should include it; if in our opinion it was not likely to, we should leave it out. Or the story of the cat might in itself seem sufficiently amusing to be inserted as a purposed *longueur*, so as to give the idea of the passage of time. ... It may be more amusing to read the story of a cat with your missing dinner than to read: "A fortnight elapsed. ..." Or it might be better after all to write boldly: "Mr. Slack, after a fortnight had elapsed, remarked one day very querulously: 'That smell seems to get worse instead of better.' "

SELECTION (SPEECHES)

That last would be compromise, for it would be narration instead of rendering: it would be far *better* to give an idea of the passage of time by picturing a cat with a cod's head, but the length of the story must be considered. Sometimes to render anything at all in a given space will take up too much room—even to render the effect and delivery of a speech. Then just boldly

and remorselessly you must relate and *risk* the introduction of
yourself as author, with the danger that you may destroy all the
illusion of the story.

Conrad and the writer would have agreed that the ideal rendering of Mr. Slack's emotions would be as follows:

"A scrawny, dark-brown neck, with an immense Adam's apple
quivering over the blue stripes of a collar erected itself between
the sunflower stems above the thin oaken flats of the dividing
fence. An unbelievably long, thin gap of a mouth opened itself
beneath a black-spotted handkerchief, to say that the unspeak-
able odour was sufficient to slay all the porters in Covent Garden.
Last week it was only bad enough to drive a regiment of dragoons
into a faint. The night before the people whom he had had to
supper—I wondered who could eat any supper with any appetite
under the gaze of those yellow eyes—people, mind you, to whom
he had hoped to sell a little bit of property in the neighbourhood.
Good people. With more than a little bit in the bank. People
whose residence would give the whole neighbourhood a lift. They
had asked if he liked going out alone at night with so many undiscovered murders about. . . . 'Undiscovered murders!' he went on
repeating as if the words gave him an intimate sense of relief. He
concluded with the phrase: 'I *don't* think!' "

That would be a very fair *rendering* of part of an episode: it
would have the use of getting quite a lot of Mr. Slack in; but you
might want to get on towards recounting how you had the lucky
idea of purchasing shares in a newspaper against which Mr. Slack
had counselled you. . . . And you might have got Mr. Slack in
already!

The rendering in fact of speeches gave Conrad and the writer
more trouble than any other department of the novel whatever.
It introduced at once the whole immense subject of under what
convention the novel is to be written. For whether you tell it
direct and as author—which is the more difficult way—or whether
you put it into the mouth of a character—which is easier by far
but much more cumbersome—the question of reporting or rendering speeches has to be faced. To pretend that any character or

any author writing directly can remember whole speeches with all their words for a matter of twenty-four hours, let alone twenty-four years, is absurd. The most that the normal person carries away of a conversation after even a couple of hours is just a salient or characteristic phrase or two, and a mannerism of the speaker. Yet, if the reader stops to think at all, or has any acuteness whatever, to render Mr. Slack's speech directly: "Thet there odour is enough to do all the porters in Common Gorden in. Lorst week it wouldn' no more 'n 'v sent a ole squad of tinwiskets barmy on the crumpet..." and so on through an entire monologue of a page and a half, must set the reader at some point or other wondering, how the author or the narrator can possibly, even if they were present, have remembered every word of Mr. Slack's long speech. Yet the object of the novelist is to keep the reader entirely oblivious of the fact that the author exists—even of the fact that he is reading a book. This is of course not possible to the bitter end, but a reader *can* be rendered very engrossed, and the nearer you can come to making him entirely insensitive to his surroundings, the more you will have succeeded.

Then again, directly reported speeches in a book do move very slowly; by the use of indirect locutions, together with the rendering of the effects of other portions of speech, you can get a great deal more into a given space. There is a type of reader that likes what is called conversations—but that type is rather the reader in an undeveloped state than the reader who has read much. So, wherever practicable, we used to arrange speeches much as in the paragraph devoted to Mr. Slack above. But quite often we compromised and gave passages of direct enough speech.

This was one of the matters as to which the writer was more uncompromising than was Conrad. In the novel which he did at last begin on his forty-first birthday there will be found to be hardly any direct speech at all, and probably none that is more than a couple of lines in length. Conrad indeed later arrived at the conclusion that, a novel being in the end a matter of convention—and in the beginning too for the matter of that, since what are type, paper, bindings and all the rest, but matters of agreement and convenience—you might as well stretch convention a little farther, and postulate that your author or your narrator is a person of a prodigious memory for the spoken. He had one minute passion with regard to conversations: he could not bear the repetition of 'he said's and 'she said's, and would spend agitated hours in chasing those locutions out of his or our pages and substituting: 'he replied,' 'she ejaculated,' 'answered Mr. Verloc' and the like. The writer was less moved by this consideration: it seemed to him that you could employ the words 'he said' as often as you like, accepting them as being unnoticeable, like 'a,' 'the' 'his' 'her,' or 'very.'

CONVERSATIONS

One unalterable rule that we had for the rendering of conversations—for genuine conversations that are an exchange of thought, not interrogatories or statements of fact—was that no speech of one character should ever answer the speech that goes before it. This is almost invariably the case in real life where few people listen, because they are always preparing their own next speeches. When, of a Saturday evening, you are conversing over the fence with your friend Mr. Slack, you hardly notice that he tells you he has seen an incredibly coloured petunia at a market-gardener's, because you are dying to tell him that you have determined to turn author to the extent of writing a letter on local politics to the newspaper of which, against his advice, you have become a large shareholder.

He says: "Right down extraordinary that petunia was——"

You say: "What would you think now of my . . ."

He says: "Diamond-shaped stripes it had, blue-black and salmon. . . ."

You say: "I've always thought I had a bit of a gift. . . ."

Your daughter Millicent interrupts: "Julia Gower has got a pair of snake-skin shoes. She bought them at Wiston and Willocks's."

You miss Mr. Slack's next two speeches in wondering where Millicent got that bangle on her wrist. You will have to tell her more carefully than ever that she must *not* accept presents from

Tom, Dick and Harry. By the time you have come out of that reverie Mr. Slack is remarking:

"I said to him use turpentine and sweet oil, three parts to two. What do you think?"

SURPRISE

We agreed that the one quality that gave interest to Art was the quality of surprise. That is very well illustrated in the snatch of conversation just given. If you reported a long speech of Mr. Slack's to the effect that he was going to enter some of his petunias for the local flower show and those, with his hydrangeas and ornamental sugar-beet, might well give him the Howard Cup for the third time, in which case it would become his property out and out. He would then buy two silver and cut-glass epergnes one to stand on each side of the Cup on his sideboard. He always did think that a touch of silver and cut glass. . . . If, after that you gave a long speech of your own: after, naturally, you had added a few commonplaces as a politeness to Mr. Slack: if you gave a long speech in which with modesty you dwelt on the powers of observation and of the pen that you had always considered yourself to possess, and in which you announced that you certainly meant to write a letter to the paper in which you had shares—on the statuary in the façade of the new town hall which was an offence to public decency . . . And if in addition to that you added a soliloquy from your daughter Millicent to the effect that she intended to obtain on credit from your bootmakers, charging them to your account, a pair of scarlet morocco shoes with two-inch heels with which to go joy-riding on the Sunday with a young actor who played under the name of Hildebrand Hare and who had had his portrait in your paper. . . . If you gave all these long speeches one after the other you might be aware of a certain dullness when you re-read that *compte rendu*. . . . But if you carefully broke up petunias, statuary, and flower-show motives and put them down in little shreds one contrasting with the other, you would arrive at something much more coloured, animated, life-like and interesting and you would convey a profoundly significant lesson as to the self-engrossment of humanity. Into that live scene you could then drop the piece of news that you wanted to convey and so you would carry the chapter a good many stages forward.

Here, again, compromise must necessarily come in: there must come a point in the dramatic working up of every scene in which the characters do directly answer each other, for a speech or for two or three speeches. It was in this department, as has already been pointed out, that Conrad was matchless and the writer very deficient. Or, again, a point may come in which it is necessary—in which at least it is to take the line of least resistance—to report directly a whole tremendous effort of eloquence as ebullient as an oration by Mr. Lloyd George on the hymns of the Welsh nation. For there are times when the paraphernalia of indirect speech, interruptions and the rest retard your action too much. Then they must go: the sense of reality must stand down before the necessity to get on.

But, on the whole, the indirect, interrupted method of handling interviews is invaluable for giving a sense of the complexity, the tantalisation, the shimmering, the haze, that life is. In the pre-war period the English novel began at the beginning of a hero's life and went straight on to his marriage without pausing to look aside. This was all very well in its way, but the very great objection could be offered against it that such a story was too confined to its characters and, too self-centredly, went on, *in vacuo*. If you are so set on the affair of your daughter Millicent with the young actor that you forget that there *are* flower shows and town halls with nude statuary your intellect will appear a thing much more circumscribed than it should be. Or, to take a larger matter. A great many novelists have treated of the late war in terms solely of the war: in terms of pip-squeaks, trench-coats, wire-aprons, shells, mud, dust, and sending the bayonet home with a grunt. For that reason interest in the late war is said to have died. But, had you taken part actually in those hostilities, you would know how infinitely little part the actual fighting itself took in your mentality. You would be lying on your stomach, in a beast of a funk, with an immense, horrid German barrage going on all over and round you and with hell and all let loose. But, apart from the occasional, petulant question: "When the deuce will our fellows get going and shut 'em up?" your thoughts were really concentrated on something quite distant: on your daughter Millicent's hair, on the fall of the Asquith Ministry, on your financial predicament, on why your regimental ferrets kept on dying, on whether Latin is really necessary to an education, or in what way really *ought* the Authorities to deal with certain diseases. . . . You were there, but great shafts of thought from the outside, distant and unattainable world infinitely for the greater part occupied your mind.

It was that effect then, that Conrad and the writer sought to get into their work, that being Impressionism.

But these two writers were not unaware that there are other methods: they were not rigid in their own methods: they were sensible to the fact that compromise is at all times necessary in the execution of every work of art.

Let us come, then, to the eternally vexed seas of the Literary Ocean.

STYLE

We agreed on this axiom:

The first business of Style is to make work interesting: the second business of Style is to make work interesting: the third business of Style is to make work interesting: the fourth business of Style is to make work interesting: the fifth business of Style. . . .

Style, then, has no other business.

A style interests when it carries the reader along: it is then a good style. A style ceases to interest when by reason of disjointed sentences, over-used words, monotonous or jog-trot cadences, it fatigues the reader's mind. *Too* startling words, however apt, *too* just images, too great displays of cleverness are apt in the long run to be as fatiguing as the most over-used words or the most jog-trot cadences. That a face resembles a Dutch clock has been too often said; to say that it resembles a ham is inexact and conveys nothing; to say that it has the mournfulness of an old, squashed-in meat tin, cast away on a waste building lot, would be smart—but too much of that sort of thing would become a nuisance. To say that a face was cramoisy is undesirable: few people nowadays know what the word means. Its employment will make the reader marvel at the user's erudition: in thus marvelling he ceases to consider the story and an impression of vagueness or length is produced on his mind. A succession of impressions of vagueness and length render a book in the end unbearable.

There are, of course, pieces of writing intended to convey the sense of the author's cleverness, knowledge of obsolete words or power of inventing similes: with such exercises Conrad and the writer never concerned themselves.

We used to say: the first lesson that an author has to learn is that of humility. Blessed are the humble because they do not get between the reader's legs. Before everything the author must learn to suppress himself: he must learn that the first thing he has to consider is his story and the last thing that he has to consider is his story, and in between that he will consider his story.

We used to say that a passage of good style began with a fresh, usual word, and continued with fresh, usual words to the end: there was nothing more to it. When we felt that we had really got hold of the reader, with a great deal of caution we would introduce a word not common to a very limited vernacular, but that only very occasionally. Very occasionally indeed: practically never. Yet it is in that way that a language grows and keeps alive. People get tired of hearing the same words over and over again. . . . It is again a matter for compromise.

Our chief masters in style were Flaubert and Maupassant: Flaubert in the greater degree, Maupassant in the less. In about the proportion of a sensible man's whisky and soda. We stood as it were on those hills and thence regarded the world. We remembered long passages of Flaubert: elaborated long passages in his spirit and with his cadences and then translated them into passages of English as simple as the subject under treatment would bear. We remembered short, staccato passages of Maupassant: invented short staccato passages in his spirit and then translated them into English as simple as the subject would bear. Differing subjects bear differing degrees of simplicity: To apply exactly the same timbre of language to a dreadful interview between a father and a daughter as to the description of a child's bedroom at night is impracticable because it is unnatural. In thinking of the frightful scene with your daughter Millicent which ruined your life, town councillor and parliamentary candidate though you had become, you will find that your mind employs a verbiage quite different from that which occurs when you remember Millicent asleep, her little mouth just slightly opened, her toys beside the shaded night-light.

Our vocabulary, then, was as simple as was practicable. But there are degrees of simplicity. We employed as a rule in writing the language that we employed in talking the one to the other. When we used French in speaking we tried mentally to render in English the least literary equivalent of the phrase. We were, however, apt to employ in our conversation words and periphrases that are not in use by, say, financiers. This was involuntary, we imagining that we talked simply enough. But later a body of younger men with whom the writer spent some years would say, after dinner: "Talk like a book, H.... Do talk like a book!" The writer would utter some speeches in the language that he employed when talking with Conrad: but he never could utter more than a sentence or two at a time. The whole mess would roar with laughter and, for some minutes, would render his voice inaudible.

If you will reflect on the language you then employed—and the writer—you will find that it was something like: "Cheerio, old bean. The beastly Adjutant's Parade is at five ack emma. Will you take my Johnnie's and let me get a real good fug in my downy bug walk? I'm fair blind to the wide to-night." That was the current language then and, in the earlier days of our conversations, some equivalent with which we were unacquainted must normally have prevailed. That we could hardly have used in our books, since within a very short time such languages become incomprehensible. Even to-day the locution 'ack emma' is no longer used and the expression 'blind to the wide' is incomprehensible—the very state is unfamiliar—to more than half the English-speaking populations of the globe.

So we talked and wrote a Middle-High-English of as unaffected a sort as would express our thoughts. And that was all that there really was to our 'style.' Our greatest admiration for a stylist in any language was given to W. H. Hudson of whom Conrad said that his writing was like the grass that the good God made to grow and when it was there you could not tell how it came.

Carefully examined a good—an interesting—style will be found to consist in a constant succession of tiny, unobservable surprises. If you write: "His range of subject was very wide and his conversation very varied and unusual; he could rouse you with his perorations or lull you with his periods; therefore his conversation met with great appreciation and he made several fast friends"— you will not find the world very apt to be engrossed by what you have set down. The results will be different if you put it: "He had the power to charm or frighten rudimentary souls into an aggravated witch-dance; he could also fill the small souls of the pilgrims with bitter misgivings: he had one devoted friend at least, and he had conquered one soul in the world that was neither rudimentary nor tainted with self-seeking."

Or, let us put the matter in another way. The catalogue of an ironmonger's store is uninteresting as literature because things in it are all classified and thus obvious: the catalogue of a farm sale is more interesting because things in it are contrasted. No one would for long read: Nails, drawn wire, ½ inch, per lb. . . . ; nails do., ¾ inch, per lb. . . . ; nails, do., inch, per lb. . . . But it is often not disagreeable to read desultorily "*Lot* 267. Pair rabbit gins. *Lot* 268, Antique powder flask. *Lot* 269, Malay Kris. *Lot* 270, Set of six sporting prints by Herring. *Lot* 271, Silver caudle cup . . . for that, as far as it goes, has the quality of surprise.

That is, perhaps, enough about Style. This is not a technical manual, and at about this point we arrive at a region in which the writer's memory is not absolutely clear as to the points on which he and Conrad were agreed. We made in addition an infinite number of experiments, together and separately in points of style and cadence. The writer, as has been said, wrote one immense book entirely in sentences of not more than ten syllables. He read the book over. He found it read immensely long. He went through it all again. He joined short sentences: he introduced relative clauses: he wrote in long sentences that had a gentle sonority and ended with a dying fall. The book read less long. Much less long. * * *

Conrad then, never wrote a true short story, a matter of two or three pages of minutely considered words, ending with a smack ... with what the French call a *coup de canon*. His stories were always what for lack of a better phrase one has to call 'long-short' stories. For these the form is practically the same as that of the novel. Or, to avoid the implication of saying that there is only one form for the novel, it would be better to put it that the form of long-short stories may vary as much as may the form for novels. The short story of Maupassant, of Tchekhov or even of the late O. Henry is practically stereotyped—the introduction of a character in a word or two, a word or two for atmosphere, a few paragraphs for story, and then, click! a sharp sentence that flashes the illumination of the idea over the whole.

This Conrad—and for the matter of that, the writer—never so much as attempted, either apart or in collaboration. The reason for this lies in all that is behind the mystic word 'justification.' Before everything a story must convey a sense of inevitability: that which happens in it must seem to be the only thing that could have happened. Of course a character may cry: "If I had then acted differently how different everything would now be." The problem of the author is to make his then action the only action that character could have taken. It must be inevitable, because of his character, because of his ancestry, because of past illness or on account of the gradual coming together of the thousand small circumstances by which Destiny, who is inscrutable and august, will push into one certain predicament. Let us illustrate:

In the rendering of your long friendship with, and ultimate bitter hostility towards, your neighbour Mr. Slack who had a greenhouse painted with Cox's aluminium paint you will, if you wish to get yourself in with the scrupulousness of a Conrad, have to provide yourself, in the first place, with an ancestry at least as far back as your grandparents. To account for your own stability of character and physical robustness you will have to give yourself two dear old grandparents in a lodge at the gates of a great nobleman: if necessary you will have to give them a brightly polished copper kettle simmering on a spotless hob, with silhouettes on each side of the mantel: in order to account for the lamentable procedure of your daughter Millicent you must provide yourself with an actress- or gipsy-grandmother. Or at least with a French one. This grandmother will have lived, unfortunately unmarried, with someone of eloquence—possibly with the great Earl-Prime Minister at whose gates is situated the humble abode of your other grandparents—at any rate she will have lived with someone from whom you will have inherited your eloquence. From her will have descended the artistic gifts to which the reader will owe your admirable autobiographic novel. If you have any physical weakness, to counterbalance the robustness of your other grandparents, you will provide your mother, shortly before your birth, with an attack of typhoid fever, due to a visit to Venice in company with your father, who was a gentleman's courier in the famliy in which your mother was a lady's maid. Your father, in order to be a courier, will have had, owing to his illegitimacy, to live abroad in very poor circumstances. The very poor circumstances will illustrate the avarice of his statesman father—an avarice which will have descended to you in the shape of that carefulness in money matters that, reacting on the detrimental tendencies inherited by Millicent from her actress-grandmother, so lamentably influences your daughter's destiny.

And of course there will have to be a great deal more than that, always supposing you to be as scrupulous as was Conrad in this matter of justification. For Conrad—and for the matter of that the writer—was never satisfied that he had really and sufficiently got his characters in: he was never convinced that he had convinced the reader, this accounting for the great lengths of some of his books. He never introduced a character, however subsidiary, without providing that character with ancestry and hereditary characteristics, or at least with home surroundings—always supposing that character had any influence on the inevitability of the story. Any policeman who arrested any character must be 'justified' because the manner in which he effected the arrest, his mannerisms, his vocabulary and his voice, might have a permanent effect on the psychology of the prisoner. The writer remembers Conrad using almost those very words during the discussion of the plot of the *Secret Agent*.

This method, unless it is very carefully handled, is apt to have the grave defect of holding a story back very considerably. You must as a rule bring the biography of a character in only after you have introduced the character: yet, if you introduce a policeman to make an arrest the rendering of his biography might well retard the action of an exciting point in the story.... It becomes then your job to arrange that the very arresting of the action is an incitement of interest in the reader, just as, if you serialise a novel, you take care to let the words *"to be continued in our next"* come in at as harrowing a moment as you can contrive.

And of course the introducing of the biography of a character may have the great use of giving contrast to the tone of the rest of the book.... Supposing that in your history of your affair with Mr. Slack you think that the note of your orderly middle-class home is growing a little monotonous, it would be very handy if you could discover that Mr. Slack had a secret, dipsomaniacal wife, confined in a country cottage under the care of a rather criminal old couple: with a few pages of biography of that old couple you could give a very pleasant relief to the sameness of your narrative. In that way the sense of reality is procured.

PHILOSOPHY, ETC.

We agreed that the novel is absolutely the only vehicle for the thought of our day. With the novel you can do anything: you can inquire into every department of life, you can explore every department of the world of thought. The one thing that you can not do is to propagandise, as author, for any cause. You must not, as author, utter any views: above all you must not fake any events. You must not, however humanitarian you may be, over-elaborate the fear felt by a coursed rabbit.

It is obviously best if you can contrive to be without views at all: your business with the world is rendering, not alteration. You have to render life with such exactitude that more specialised beings than you, learning from you what are the secret needs of humanity, may judge how many white-tiled bathrooms are, or to what extent parliamentary representation is, necessary for the happiness of men and women. * * *

PROGRESSION D'EFFET

There is just one other point. In writing a novel we agreed that every word set on paper—*every* word set on paper—must carry the story forward and, that as the story progressed, the story must be carried forward faster and faster and with more and more intensity. That is called *progression d'effet*, words for which there is no English equivalent.

One might go on to further technicalities, such as how to squeeze the last drop out of a subject. The writer has, however, given an instance of this in describing how we piled perils of the hangman's rope on the unfortunate John Kemp. To go deeper into the matter would be to be too technical. Besides enough has been said in this chapter to show you what was the character, the scrupulousness and the common sense of our hero.

There remains to add once more:

But these two writers were not unaware—were not unaware—*that there are other methods of writing novels. They were not rigid even in their own methods. They were sensible to the fact that compromise is at all times necessary to the execution of a work of art.*

The lay reader will be astonished at this repetition and at these italics. They are inserted for the benefit of gentlemen and ladies who comment on books in the Press.

LANGUAGE

It would be disingenuous to avoid the subject of language. This is the only matter on which the writer ever differed fundamentally from Conrad. It was one upon which the writer felt so deeply that, for several years, he avoided his friend's society. The pain of approaching the question is thus very great. * * *

Conrad's indictment of the English language was this, that no English word is a word: that all English words are instruments for exciting blurred emotions. 'Oaken' in French means 'made of oak wood'—nothing more. 'Oaken' in English connotes innumerable moral attributes: it will connote stolidity, resolution, honesty, blond features, relative unbreakableness, absolute unbendableness—also, made of oak.... The consequence is, that no English word has clean edges: a reader is always, for a fraction of a second, uncertain as to which meaning of the word the writer may intend. Thus, all English prose is blurred. Conrad desired to write a prose of extreme limpidity....

We may let it go at that. In later years Conrad achieved a certain fluency and a great limpidity of language—the result being the *Rover*, which strikes the writer as being a very serene and beautiful work. Conrad then regretted that, for him, all the romance of writing was gone. In between the two he made tributes to the glory of the English language by implication contemning the tongue that Flaubert used. This at the time struck the writer, at that time in a state of exhausted depression, as unforgivable—as the very betrayal of Dain by Tom Lingard.... Perhaps it was. If it were Conrad faced the fact in that book. There are predicaments that beset great Adventurers, in dark hours, in the shallows: the overtired nerve will fail.... We may well let it go at that. * * *

Ford Madox Ford, *Joseph Conrad: A Personal Remembrance* (London: Duckworth and Co., 1924), pp. 180–199, 204–208, 210–211, 214–215.

Letters to
John Galsworthy, H. G. Wells,
Herbert Read, Anthony Bertram

Ford was a strong believer in literary movements and in continual social intercourse between artists, not because he considered political or social action to be the function of literature, but because he thought that technical discussions amongst writers would bring about improved literary standards. As a result, he was always anxious to talk about writing himself, and he enjoyed living in literary capitals. On the other hand, he also liked to live in the country where literary discussion was infrequent. At such times he therefore took to writing letters to those who sent their work to him for his consideration.

The letter to Galsworthy is a long evaluation of an early novel, Villa Rubein, *which Galsworthy published at the turn of the century under the pseudonym of John Sinjohn. That to Wells was occasioned by the publication of* Mankind in the Making, *a copy of which Wells had sent to Ford. The selections from the letters to Anthony Bertram and Sir Herbert Read were written for the most part during the early 1920's when Ford was living in Sussex. Both men had met Ford soon after the war and were encouraged by him in their literary careers. These letters all demonstrate in different ways Ford's methods as a personal critic, that is as a man who painstakingly attempted to help other writers attain the standards he believed in.*

ALDINGTON,
HYTHE, KENT.

MY DEAR GALSWORTHY,—Excuse my writing by machine; Christina* at this moment monopolizes the only pen there is in the house. I have just finished reading the *Villa Rubein,* with a great deal of pleasure and with my interest sustained to the last page—to the last word, even, and that is the great thing, it seems to me. I don't write as a critic, which I am not, but as a fellow craftsman who looks at a piece of work and wonders what he would have made of it himself. The mere writing is of course all right, lucid and excellent, very level, and felicitous in places—quite beyond the ordinary. Of course "writing" isn't very much; one has or hasn't it just as one has or hasn't a sense of smell; one can acquire it, but you have it and it's just as well not to have to worry, I mean rather for the reader than the writer. What however is essential for me is the "distinction" of the book; that is there beyond doubt and that *is* the essential, is why I can read the *Villa Rubein* when I can't read more than three or four of the other books that the weary year brings out. I say distinction, but there is not any word to express exactly what I mean; perhaps "temperament" comes nearer the mark. When one reads a book one is always wondering more or less what kind of a man the writer is —as writer be it said. In this case the writer is all right; speaks with a right sort of voice; has things to say worth the listening to; has a philosophy and finds expression for it. I don't mean to say that the *Villa Rubein* is a flawless masterpiece. It isn't of course. But by reason of those qualities one is made to think that the writer stands not infinite distances away from the small band in which the elect keep apart; that, given chance, luck, exemption from death, weariness, disease, old age and power to keep his face steadfastly towards the light that he has seen, the writer ought to make his way across the rough ground where the light shines on hillocks, ant-heaps, mounds, and stretch of stubble and plough, into the very circle of the light itself.

This is monstrous, patronizing, fine writing and it seems neces-

*Ford's first daughter was named Christina.

sary to postulate that I don't write as one warming my hands by that fire and calling out: "Keep on, young man: a little to the right ... now, a little to the left ... mind the broken bottles or you'll cut your toes...." Rather—looking towards the fire too, but from a slightly different angle, I think I see reflected light on obstacles that perhaps you do not see, and give a friendly hail.

There isn't, in fact, any doubt that you have the *right* to write, and I who am a jealous Trade Unionist cannot pay you a greater compliment or mean it more sincerely. As a matter of fact I only accord it to about a twohandsful fingers of others, if so many. That being said, I will go on to what *I* should have desired to get into the book—over and above what it has—if it were my own work. In the first place what I am always striving to get at is:

> The ultimate reasons of the futile earth
> And crawling swarms of men ...

I mean that I want to know the writer's attitude towards the Post, if not Super Natural. I don't think, whatever you have that takes the place of my Destiny—that whatever it is has enough of a show. Mind you, one asks for something to take the place of the Trinity and the Finger of God, one wants to feel after reading a book: this happened because it was absolutely impossible for it to have happened otherwise. One may or may not feel this about the *Villa Rubein*. I think myself that, given your characters, your events are all right. But that is not enough. One wants to feel, not that the Finger of Chance is the ultimate factor of the lives set before us, but that all the little chances and all of the few great haps of a life are only manifestations of the only thing that is worth the thinking about ... of cause and effect. She was so and so because of her heredity; he so and so because of the hardships of his life acting like certain acids on certain salts. Yes, yes, *I* know it because I look out for it; but what you have to do is to prove, to the man who does not look out, that they could not possibly have *done* but what they did: because, in the scheme of things as you see it and (what is more essential) as you have hypnotized them into seeing it, such and such contacts of *a* and *b* make $a^2 + 2ab + b^2$. It is all there in the book, the Cornish-

Devonshire ancestry, the contact of a hunger-weakened mind with Russian Nihilism.... But the points are not *quite* made, the destiny of it not *quite* brought out after being put in. One has to stop and think. Now a perfect County Council puts sign-posts at its ventways because the roads are made for country-people primarily and only secondarily for tourists furnished with good, bad or indifferent maps.

Then again: there is not enough vinegar in the salad. You are too kind, too deferential to your characters; you haven't enough contempt, enough of the *saeva indignatio*. Perhaps you have not enough aloofness from them; have drawn them too much from the life. Catholicity is the first necessity of a writer on men; but there must also be room for the reaction. Turgenev had plenty, plenty, plenty of human sympathy, but all the time he was putting in his Bazarovs and his young men and old, his maids and matrons, he knew that he, as Creator, was infinitely above them, and at times that peeped out. Let it come out in your work too. You too are miles above any of the characters you create; you must be or you could not create them. Keep that always in your mind; it is one of the defects of your qualities, of your temperament. It is true there are no villains in the world; you have the sense to see that I, who am an Anarchist, a destroyer, am not, when all the shouting is over, ethically a bit worse than Mr. Cecil Rhodes who is an Empire Builder. I am not a bit better. I am just as futile, just as human, deserve spitting on just as much. Yes, spit at them sometimes, because your Christian (why Xtian, which seems to me to be the *masculine* of Xtine?) your Xtian would most probably not appreciate one bit the technical merits of the *Villa Rubein*. Put more shadow into it; there *is* more shadow. One's fellow-creatures are despicable as well as pathetic; one is oneself, but that doesn't come into the story.

This is of course vastly *ex parte—ex mea parte—*and there is more to be said for your sympathy than for my disdain. I was thinking, when I was reading your *Villa Rubein*, of a girl I once treated of; a girl of much the same character; very charming; a girl I am very fond of in my way. I took hold of that young woman and ran in every bit of her charm I could think of and then smashed in all the repulsion I could think of; the boredom of her, the washed-out look of a morning, the inevitable nerves, the hysteria—and yet she was a charming girl.

Your Xtian is better done than that; she isn't one side pink muslin and the other black and purple checked cloth; it's not with her I'm quarreling. Indeed I'm not quarrelling with any of the characters except perhaps Greta who is all charm. To me she is an undesirable; the danger with children is that they set for the reader very much the tone of the book. One is inclined to say: "Ah, this man, this writer, only sees the charm and not the hideous worry and bother of the dressing and washing, the Latin lessons and the rest. He is only a visitor in this House of Life." A child like that is a danger throughout; she takes up room; introduces dangerous touches of naïveté into scenes where the nerves are a-tremble for the saving of a situation (I am thinking of her remark about bats in the scene in Harz's unscrewed studio) and so on. I can't for a moment say that she is a superfluous character, she is, on the contrary, very necessary, for the story, for relief and so on. But I cavil at her as I did at the idyllic touches in the Cosmopolitan because she takes up too much space and has worried me a little in the progression *d'effet* of the end of the scenes with Treffry—very fine work that, all, by the bye.

Looking back I find I have attacked you somewhat viciously in parts of the story. I did not mean to do that, but rather to use the defects—or what seemed to me defects, as pegs to hang theoretic disquisitions upon art, as I see it in my limited field of view. As I said before, my dear fellow, you gave the right personality, your work has undeniable distinction. The *Villa Rubein* seems to me a little weak in form and in other essentials. But it shows very plainly that *you* are not weak in the essentials and, as I said before, I read the book with real pleasure who read hardly any books with any pleasure, except those of three or four men whom you know very well. Because it is distinction, and again distinction and again distinction that one wants, and that you have.

Pardon this inordinate length. I have rattled on as if I were talking to a better listener than I deserve and I am a dogmatic cuss at best; also a typewriter lends itself to excesses because, not being able to amend words, one has to amplify until one flounders and flounders, over boots and over spurs.—Yours,

FORD MADOX HUEFFER.

Letter quoted in H. V. Marrot, *The Life and Letters of John Galsworthy* (London: Heinemann Ltd., 1935), pp. 121–124.

THE BUNGALOW,
WINCHELSEA.
1903

MY DEAR WELLS,
* * *

By the bye: I lament to see you fall into the error of upholding "Elizabethanism." That sort of thing is the curse of modern English. What we want is to use our vernacular so skilfully that words, precious or obsolete, will not stick out or impede a reader. You practice that well enough yourself: why seek to lead astray the young? Or why fix the limit at "Elizabethanism"? Why not uphold the "Well-wenning[?] by the wan waters" of the late W. Morris? Or why not pepper your page all over—as alas I do, for my sins, with foreign words? I did think that you at least had a hearty contempt for the British classic—Elizabethans! Oh Lord: what single one of them, except Shakespeare, cd. express a clear thought clearly? No, sir: their vocabulary seems better than ours because we are creatures of association—precisely because we consider a ploughed field "Nature." We have been taught to consider Elizabethan words as "poetical"—and so we do. And we all of us have in us a little touch of the pedant: we like to twist things round to show off. But really it's much better to write "not pertinent" and to keep "impertinent" for its present use. If you don't you will have to use some periphrasis to express the latter sense. If you will reconsider the matter you will see that slang is an excellent thing. (Elizabethan writing is mostly slang.) And as soon as is practicable we shd. get into our pages every slang word that doesn't (in our selective ears) ring too horribly ... We must do that or we shall die, we and our language.

Again you undervalue Latin: it's not a thing valuable as making a Don turn up his nose, but it's of inestimable use as helping us to acquire foreign languages and to understand our own without the help of dictionaries. I really think one might as well set out to make laws without having seen a man, or sociology without the intimate historic sense, as easily as learn any of the Romance or quasi-Romance languages without a knowledge of Latin. Even Greek is useful to this end: how otherwise do I remember such a word as "cacodylate" which I have heard only once in my life—or rhododendra or UTOPIA?

Consider, oh my friend, these points—for, very firstly, you make the sense of language so important a part of your scheme. What we want is rather to cultivate that "sense" than to increase our vocabularies with obsolete words that are attractive mainly because they are *allusive*.

Letter in the H. G. Wells Collection, University of Illinois Library.

RED FORD
HURSTON
PULBOROUGH
11/6/20

(TO HERBERT READ)
* * *

No, not a bit have I grown tired of talk about books—and youth is a golden thing. "Education Sentimentale" is Stonehenge; but *What Maisie Knew* is certainly Stratford on Avon (Though God forbid that the Old Man should hear me say so!) *Le Rouge et le Noir* is the perfect thing upon which to model one's style, if one does not model it on *Coeur Simple*—which is worth a wilderness of apes, monkeys, Times Supplement Reviewers and almost every other thing in the world. . . . But the *Real Thing* is nearly as good. Only Henry was just a *little* provincial-pharisaic, whereas Flaubert was so huge, untidy, generous—and such a worker! Still, as someone or other said, L'un et L'autre se disent and if you aren't in the mood for Stonehenge the Birthplace is a very good substitute—and Henri Beyle, perhaps, a better still.

I rejoice in your felicity; it is good to be happy and keep bees —good for others as well as yourself. And a Novel! I am really glad to hear of that. Why not come here and read it or talk it over. It gives one a lift sometimes to talk of one's stuff.

RED FORD
HURSTON
PULBOROUGH
30/6/20

DEAR READ;
* * *

If you want to talk about and scheme out a novel it is—so I have found by long, long, long experience—better to begin it early. If you talk to a bloke to whose judgment you feel inclined to pay some deference the less you have actually written the better; because, if there is a lot put down it is apt to make one obstinate in its defence; the natural law of laziness comes in. Whereas if one talks of a project one sees it crystallise in various shapes as the conference proceeds and one has a more open choice... I mean to say: there is the whole open question of Impersonalism to discuss. And then: the house is open to you: You can come and talk about it at practically every stage, if you want to—except that, during August we shall be plastering and papering at Cooper's; during September, moving in and during October and November resting from our labours in one Metropolis or other, supposing us to have the car-hire left to get away. * * *

RED FORD
24/7/20

DEAR READ:
* * *

And glad, too that you have begun your novel. That's it really, get your formula and then pioche away with your head beneath the blanket. Then look up for a couple of months and take stock of results. If your formula is all right you will then begin to see, as it were the spitloching of a Form and the rest will be straight-forward spade work.

And there is one very great material advantage in having the line really planned out: it means that one can sit down after interruptions—which in your case are diurnal—just carry straight on because the work has been done in one's head. Whereas, if one has neither formula nor Form, when one comes to the Pen one spends immeasurable time in the effort to catch on or to invent.

COOPERS,
BEDHAM
NR FITTLEWORTH
SUSSEX
19/9/20

MY DEAR READ:
* * *

I don't know that I am the most sympathetic person to come to for one inclined to desert the practice of novel writing for the indulgence in metaphysics. For, firstly, I never knew what meta-physics were and, secondly, I have for years and years and years held that the only occupation to which a serious man could seri-ously put himself was the writing of novels—if only because, in all the varied domains to which the very limited human intelligence applies itself this is the only one that is practically unexplored—the only one in which it is possible to find a New Form. And it is only the finding of a New Form that is a worthy occupation.

So at least I see it—and the immense advantage that the Novel has over the frivolous apparition called the Serious Book—is that, if you are really serious enough you can say what you like. . . I mean that you can ram all the metaphysics in the world into it and it can still be a fine work of art. . . Or all the Strategy, Biol-ogy, Bibliography and Philately that count.

I don't see what Yorkshire has to do with it—except that all

Yorkshire people, as I have known them, are singularly lazy and singularly self-sufficient (Present Company, of course, always excepted!) My friend Marwood,* as you say, was a case in point: he had the clear intelligence of a poet but, rather than trespass on his own shyness and shamefacedness, he would spend days making corrections out of his head on the Margins of the Encyclopaedia Britannica. He just—peace to his ashes—wanted to bolster up his self-conceit to himself (He didn't boast of the achievement to any other soul), and, of course, to remain tres grand seigneur, Marwood of Busby, and so on.... That is at the bottom of most Yorkshire dislike of the Arts—a sort of shyness and love of ease! Your county folk see a Poet performing coram populo! They say to themselves: We dare not appear in public: they say aloud: That is a contemptible fellow! And gradually their public utterances become themselves and they end as sidesmen at the local Bethel! And conceal the Venus of Milo, as she used to be concealed in Leeds Art Gallery, behind aspidistras!

Don't let yourself undergo that hardening process; it is a very stupid one; and try to forget that you come from the Sheeres at all... Whitechapel is really a better lieu de naissance...

Of course I see you aiming at becoming another Henri Beyle: but it is a miserable ambition... Learn of Stendahl all you can—and there is, if you do not happen to be Middleton Murry—an immense deal to learn in an artistic sense... But don't model yourself on him... I can imagine no more terrible being to himself than a Yorkshireman, true to type, and modelling himself on Mr. Beyle!—The end would be the most horribly costive neurastheniac you can imagine, with incredible sex obsessions sedulously concealed, swaddled up to the ears in red flannel for fear of draughts, and with more hypochondrias and phobias than to be found in all Freud, Jung and the late Marie Bashkirtseff put together... And with a yellow, furred tongue, and a morgue britannique beyond belief...

No, try not to become that... You may not like novel writing

*Arthur Marwood, who died in about 1916, was later used by Ford as a model for Christopher Tietjens, the central figure of the *Parade's End* series of novels.

but it would be a good thing to stick to it so as to avoid turning your soul into a squirrel in a revolving cage... Still, it is not for me to interfere with the destiny of others and, if you will you will.

You are unjust, rather to Conrad... He is a Pole, and, being a Pole is Elizabethan. He has done an immense deal for the Nuvvle in England—not so much as I, no doubt, but then that was not his job, and he is of the generation before mine. I learned all I know of Literature from Conrad—and England has learned all it knows of Literature from me... I do not mean to say that Conrad did not learn a great deal from me when we got going; I daresay he learned more actual stuff from me than I of him. But, but for him, I should have been a continuation of DANTE GABRIEL ROSSETTI—and think of the loss that would have been to you young things.... And think what English Literature would be without Conrad and James... There would be nothing!

You may say that Conrad's prose is always a Ceremonial Parade of words, with a General Salute and a March Past twice in every chapter... "And her mute glance conveyed to me the silence of an ineffable love; the glory of pain which is without end; a profound and inalterable...."... and so on... And Trench Boots (See A.Ci. I. 99946781, 1897!) must not be worn on ceremonial parades! That is true... But you *must* have gallant and splendid shots at Prose with a Panache... Yorkshire needs them more than anything else in the world! More than anything! Because we can always do the "A-Oh!," reticence stunt! Nothing, nothing, is easier... And then we call it selection... But Conrad is Renaissance, because Poland is a 16th century nation—and we want all the Renaissance stuff we can get in these islands... A great Master!

Letters in the possession of the owner, Sir Herbert Read. Portions of these letters are included in Read's *Annals of Innocence and Experience* (London: Faber and Faber, Ltd., 1940).

COOPERS
BEDHAM
FITTLEWORTH
SUSSEX
14/8/22

MY DEAR BERTRAM;
* * *

I *can't* write much about your stories now, for I am sick and tired of writing about writing, having suddenly determined to get a real move on with my History of British Literature. But certainly you, Bertram, have in this last batch improved a great deal on what you shewed me down here: the haunted house one is quite another matter (from what it then was!) and, with an illuminative phrase here and there you might make something *quite* good of it.

Felicity Chimney is a much more ambitious matter: the only thing that is wrong with it is that it is too written. You try—literally!—talking as you write for a month or so and, after that, try writing as you find you talk. I believe you would then find words have quite another savour. Reading French—the best French—is nearly as good if you try here and there to translate as you go along. Nearly as good but not quite, though it does not make you so personally unpopular as if you try to talk like a book to your intimates. Best of all is to combine the two processes. I am really quite serious in writing that.

What is wrong with your style is that you combine two vocabularies, our spoken language with the English-literary jargon and the introduction of one type of word into a passage of the other type *blurs* the effect tremendously. And, if you intend to go on writing stories with, for basis, metaphysical ideas you can not afford a blur anywhere. You may be as chary, as delicate, as you like in the amount of matter you vouchsafe, but what you do give must be extravagantly clear. And that clearness dies the moment there is in the reader's mind the least hesitation about a word. For, remember! If a narrator is telling a story—and particularly if the story be a narrative of personal adventure—the words he uses will be enormously powerful sidelights thrown onto his character. They can be used to illuminate a man's history, his tastes, his sensitiveness to his surroundings—innumerable things. Supposing a man of whom you knew nothing of you said to you suddenly: at a tea-fight: "This room is more like a J.C.R. than a lady's drawing room!" You might work out a great deal about his character, tastes and past. Of course the Reader is not a detective all through; but he is that, instinctively and unwittingly, to the measure of his knowledge, as soon as he takes up a Short Story. So that, my dear Watson . . . . * * *

GRAND HOTEL PORTE
ST. AGRÈVE
ARDÈCHE
FRANCE
4/7/23

DEAR BERTRAM;
* * *

This however is only a note. I can't consider "subjects" quietly and write about 'em—wh. is what you probably want—because I am in the middle of "subjects" of my own wh. exhaust all the small brain I've got. But—règle générale I think it's more practical to begin with an action or incident and spin your subject round it than to begin with a "subject" and work architectonics out of it. Every incident—anecdote—has of necessity subject, atmosphere and the inevitabilities of character behind it. I believe that's really the sound way to elaborate a novel: think of an anecdote: double it: halve it: add three. . . and so on as we used to set problems at school. But there's no universal formula: only that's the least *boring* way for oneself!

CAP BRUN
15/10/35

MY DEAR BERTRAM,

I have now read—but indeed I did a week or so ago—*Men Adrift* with a great deal of pleasure—pleasure because it was fun

reading it and at being able to think that you have found a form
that is really suited to you and have managed your subject with
a great deal of skill. It is certainly a great advance on anything
else you have ever done and I really congratulate you. The book
is full of good things, moving steadily forward altogether—and,
if the progression of effect doesn't end in final illumination that
is, I suppose, because there is no illumination to be found in the
state of being adrift.

But I imagine—indeed I am pretty sure—that when you do get
hold of a really good subject that is really suited to you you will
now do something authentic. The Christ progression is, you
know, really too *vieux jeu* and too provincially Middle Class
English. You *must* shake that off, if only because it is a source of
continual slackness. When the Englishman—who is almost never
a Christian but always, or almost always, a Christ-ist—takes the
Christ saga in hand it means that he is treating a subject that is
already more than half written for him and, being able to do
without invention in that Particular, he permits himself to
slacken off in all the Christ-cum-Magi or Christ-cum-whatever-
else-he-pleases passages and then he is in the greatest danger of
going slack all over the shop. In the end he is really only embroi-
dering on a fairy tale—and there are now in the world so many
people who don't even know the fairy tale, that at once you get
provincialism. We as Englishmen have gone on for long imagining that if we as individuals model ourselves on the English ideal
of the Redeemer we shall have a good time—for so long that we
expect the Redeemer to touch his forelock like a good footman
and give us supernatural market tips and advantages even when
we are doing no more than write a novel. The process is wanting
in respect to the Son of God.

Obviously you have carried the matter a little further than
that—but to attain the really authentic you must cut loose altogether from that sort of thing; you must give up being a Christist
and become a Christian or something else that is fierce and bitter
as Christians have to be. Christianity isn't you know a Sunday
supper with the maids given the evening off: it is eating flesh and
drinking blood. When you do that the legendary caboodle—all

of it—grows so dim that is is unrecognisable and can't be used for progressions of effect in books. If you had been—as we've just been for the last few days—in Geneva what I mean would appear to you with startling effect.

But objecting to a fellow's subject isn't objecting to his texture or his writing or anything but just the subject—and subjects are extraordinarily a matter of luck, environment, accident and perhaps a little laziness or lack of having suffered. You just keep on with the same texture and writing and when you have pioché'd enough you'll get the right subject and then you will be all right right through. I am really immensely pleased and impressed with the book; the feeling of a crowd going forward like a slow tidal wave is really admirably achieved. Keep it up and you will be all right.

Letters in the possession of the owner, Anthony Bertram, Esq.

NOVELISTS AND NOVELS

Henry James

When they first met in the late 1890's in London, James simply looked upon Ford as an agreeable young man about town who could help give him a sense of English social life. The information he gained through their acquaintance was useful to him in The Wings of the Dove, *and in that book he used Ford as a physical model for Merton Densher. Later on, both men moved to Sussex where they lived in neighboring villages. Their proximity gave them opportunity for further intercourse, and for a number of years they saw each other frequently.*

Thus in 1935, when he was asked to write a series of literary portraits for the American Mercury, *later published together as* Portraits from Life, *Ford was able to combine personal anecdotes about "the Master" with his evaluation of his literary work, and to give an overall impression of James's contribution to English letters. This essay, then, is an example of Ford's critical impressionism, a type of literary criticism which is extremely difficult to write but at which he became expert by the end of his life.*

THE MASTER

I WILL begin this work with a little romance in the style of the Master—for *what* an intrigue he would have made of it if he had heard it at one of the hospitable boards where he so continually picked up what "I have always recognized on the spot as 'germs' " —the central ideas from which sprang his innumerable stories. ...And it is the innumerability of his stories rather than the involutions of his style and plots that most have struck me in re-reading the work of him who must, whether we like to acknowledge it or not, be called the great master of all us novelists of to-day.

I hasten to avert thunders from my head by saying that I know that there are thousands of novelists of to-day and here who will swear that they never read a word of Henry James—just as the first words that Mr. H. M. Tomlinson ever said to me were, "Never heard of the fellow!"—the "fellow" being Conrad. But one's master is far more an aura in the air than an admonitory gentleman with uplifted forefinger, and one learns as much by reacting against a prevailing tendency as by following in a father's footsteps. . . .

Well, then . . . I was sitting one day in my study in Winchelsea when, from beside the window, on the little verandah, I heard a male voice, softened by the intervening wall, going on and on interminably . . . with the effect of a long murmuring of bees. I had been lost in the search for one just word or other so that the gentle sound had only dreamily penetrated to my attention. When it did so penetrate and after the monologue had gone on much, much longer, a certain irritation took hold of me. Was I not the owner of the establishment? Was I not supposed by long pondering over just words and their subsequent transference to paper to add at least to the credit, if not to the resources of that establishment? Was it not, therefore, understood that chance visitors must *not* be entertained at the front door which was just beside my window? . . . The sound, however, was not harsh or disagreeable and I stood it for perhaps another ten minutes. But at last impatience overcame me and I sprang to my door.

Silhouetted against the light at the end of the little passage were the figures of one of the housemaids and of Mr. Henry James. And Mr. James was uttering the earth-shaking question:

"Would you then advise me . . . for I know that such an ornament decorates your master's establishment and you will therefore from your particular level be able to illuminate me as to the . . . ah . . . smooth functioning of such, if I may use the expression, a wheel in the domestic timepiece—always supposing that you will permit me the image, meaning that, as I am sure in this household is the case, the daily revolution of a really harmonious *chez soi* is as smooth as the passing of shadows over a dial . . . would you then advise me to have . . . in short to introduce into *my* household and employ . . . a . . . that is to say . . . a Lady Help?"

I advanced at that and, as the housemaid with a sigh of relief disappeared amongst the rustlings of her skirts, in the strongest and firmest possible terms assured Mr. James that such an adornment of the household of an illustrious and well-appointed bachelor was one that should very certainly not be employed. He sighed. He appeared worn, thin for him, dry-skinned, unspirited. His liquid and marvellous dark eyes were dulled, the skin over his aquiline nose was drawn tight. He was suffering from a domestic upheaval—his household, that for a generation had, indeed, revolved around him as quietly as the shadows on a dial, with housekeeper, butler, upper housemaid, lower housemaid, tweeny maid, knife-boy, gardener, had suddenly erupted all round him so that for some time he had been forced to content himself with the services of the knife-boy.

That meant that he had to eat in the ancient hostelry, called The Mermaid, that stood beside his door. And, his housekeeper having for thirty years and more sent up, by the imposing if bottle-nosed butler who was her husband, all Mr. James's meals without his ever having ordered a single one—being used to such a halcyon cuisine the Master had not the slightest idea of what foods agreed with him and which did not. So that everything disagreed with him and he had all the appearance of being really ill. . . . The cause of the bottle-nose had been also the occasion of the eruption, all the female servants having one day left in a body on account of the "carryings-on" of the butler, and the butler himself, together, alas, with his admirable wife, the housekeeper, having, twenty-four hours later, to be summarily and violently ejected by a sympathetic police sergeant.

So the poor Master was not only infinitely worried about finding an appropriate asylum for the butler and his wife, but had to spend long mornings and afternoons on what he called "the benches of desolation in purgatorial, if I may allow myself the word, establishments, ill-named, since no one appeared there to register themselves . . . eminently ill-named: *registry-offices* . . ." And there would be a sound like the hiss of a snake as he uttered the compound word. . . .

He would pass his time, he said, interviewing ladies all of a certain age, all of haughty—the French would say *renfrognée*—expressions, all of whom would unanimously assure him that, if they demeaned themselves merely by for an instant considering the idea of entering the household of an untitled person like himself, in such a God-forsaken end of the world as the Ancient Town of Rye, they having passed their lives in the families of never anyone less than a belted earl in mansions on Constitution Hill in the shadow of Buckingham Palace ... if they for a fleeting moment toyed with the idea, it was merely, they begged to assure him ... "forthegoodoftheirhealths." Mr. James having dallied with this sentence would utter the last words with extreme rapidity, raising his eyebrows and his cane in the air and digging the ferrule suddenly into the surface of the road. . . .

How they come back to me after a quarter of a century ... the savoured, half-humorous, half-deprecatory words, the ironically exaggerated gestures, the workings of the closely shaved lips, the halting to emphasize a point, the sudden scurryings forward, for all the world like the White Rabbit hurrying to the Queen's tea-party ... along the Rye Road, through the marshes, from Winchelsea ... I walking beside him and hardly ever speaking, in the guise of God's strong, silent Englishman—which he took me really to be. . . .

To give the romance, then, its happy ending. . . . One of the matrons of Rye had conceived the idea of lodging a dependent orphan niece in poor Mr. James's house and so had recommended him to employ a Lady Help, offering to supply herself that domestic functionary. He had consulted as to the advisability of this step all the doctors', lawyers', and parsons' wives of the neighbourhood, and in addition one of the local great ladies—I think it was Lady Maude Warrender. The commoners' ladies, loyal to the one who wanted to dispose of the dependent niece, had all said the idea was admirable. Her Ladyship was non-committal, going no further than to assure him that the great ladies of the neighbourhood would not refuse to come to tea with him in his garden —that being their, as well as his, favourite way of passing an afternoon—merely because he should shelter an unattached orphan beneath his roof. But she would go no further than that.

So, in his passion for getting, from every possible angle, light on every possible situation—including his own—he had walked over to Winchelsea to consult not only me, but any female member of my household upon whom he should chance, and had kept the appalled and agitated housemaid for a full half hour on the doorstep whilst he consulted her as to the advisability of the step he was contemplating. . . . But I soon put a stop to *that* idea. In practical matters Mr. James did me the honour to pay exact attention to my opinions—I was for him the strong, silent man of affairs.

How long his agony lasted after that I cannot say. His perturbations were so agonizing to witness that it seemed to be a matter of years. And then, one day, he turned up with a faint adumbration of jauntiness. At last he had heard of a lady who gave some promise of being satisfactory. . . . The only shadow appeared to be the nature of her present employment.

"Guess," he said, "under whose august roof she is at the moment sheltering? . . . *Je vous le donne en mille.* . . ." He started back dramatically, rolling his fine eyes, and with great speed he exclaimed:

"The Poet Laureate . . . no less a person!"

Now the Poet Laureate occupies in England a position that it is very difficult to explain. By his official situation he is something preposterous and eminent . . . and at the same time he is something obsolescent, harmless, and ridiculous. Southey, Tennyson, and Doctor Bridges have commanded personally a certain respect, but I cannot think of anyone else who was anything else than ridiculous . . . rendered ridiculous by his office. And at the time of which I am speaking the whole literary world felt outragedly that either Swinburne or Mr. Kipling ought to have been the laureate. As it was, the holder of the title was a Mr. Alfred Austin, an obscure, amiable, and harmless poetaster who wrote about manor-houses and gardens and lived in a very beautiful manor-house in a very beautiful garden.

And, two days later Mr. James turned up, radiant. He lifted both hands above his head and exclaimed:

"As the German Emperor is said to say about his moustache, *'it is accomplished.'*... Rejoice—as I am confident you will—with me, my young friend. All from now onwards shall, I am assured, be with me gas and gingerbread.... Halcyon, halcyon days. In short, ahem...." And he tapped himself lightly on the breast and assumed the air of a traveller returned from the wintry seas. "I went," he continued, "to the house of the Poet Laureate ... to the back door of course ... and interviewed a Lady who, except for one trifling—let us not say defect but let us express it 'let or hindrance' to what I will permit myself to call the perfect union, the continuing *lune de miel* ... except for that, then, she appeared the perfect, the incredible, the except for the pure-in-heart, unattainable She ... But upon delicate inquiry ... oh, I assure you, inquiry of the *most* delicate ... for the obstacle was no less than that on reckoning up the tale of her previous 'situation' ... as twenty years with the Earl of Breadalbane, thirty years with Sir Ponsonby Peregrine Perowne, forty with the Right Honourable the Lord Bishop of Tintagel and Camelot ... on reckoning up the incredible tale of years it appeared that she must be of the combined ages of Methusaleh and the insupportable Mariner—not of your friend Conrad, but of the author of *Kubla Khan*. But upon investigation it appeared that this paragon and phoenix actually was and in consequence will, to the end of recorded time, remain, exactly the same age as" ... and he took three precise, jaunty steps to rear, laid his hand over his heart and made a quick bow ... "*myself....*"

"And," he resumed, "an upper housemaid and her sister, the under housemaid, who had left me in circumstances that I was unable to fathom but that to-day are only too woefully apparent to me, having offered to return and to provide a what they call tweeny of their own choosing ... all shall for the future be as I have already adumbrated, not only gas and gingerbread, but cloves and clothes pegs and beatitude and bliss and beauty...." And so it proved.

I have taken some time over that Romance because the whole of James, the man, could be evolved from it—and a great deal of

James, the writer. For me the strongest note of all in his character was expressed in his precautions. Not his cautions, for in action, as in writing, he was not in the least cautious.

Whether for his books or life he studied every aspect of the affair on which he was engaged with extraordinary elaboration— the elaboration which he gave to every speech that he uttered. And he was a man of the most amazing vitality, inexhaustible, indefatigable. He consulted everybody from the conductor of the tram from Rye Harbour to Rye golf links, to the chauffeur of a royal automobile who, having conveyed his august master to call on the local great lady, spent a disgusted afternoon in The Mermaid expressing rancour at the fact that the stone-deaf old lady who kept the local tollgate should have refused to let her Sovereign pass through except after payment of a shilling. What exact treasures of information Mr. James can have extracted as to either the passengers to the golf links or the travelling habits of Edward VII, or what use he expected to make of that information, I do not know. But he had an extraordinary gift of exacting confidences and even confessions so that his collection of human instances must have been one of the vastest that any man ever had. It made him perhaps feel safe—or at least as safe as it was in his nature to feel. He could feel, that is to say, that he knew his own *milieu*—the coterie of titled, distinguished, and "good" people in which he and his books moved and had their beings. And in the special English sense the words "good people" does not mean the virtuous, but all the sufficiently well-born, sufficiently inconspicuous, sufficiently but not too conspicuously opulent, sufficiently but very certainly not too conspicuously intelligent and educated, that supply recruits to the ruling classes of the British Isles. . . .

Of that class he knew the lives and circumstances, at first perhaps rather superficially and with enthusiasm, and at last profoundly and with disillusionment as profound as his knowledge. . . . And it comforted him to know "things" about the lives of the innumerable not-born that surrounded the manors or the De Vere Street apartments of the people he really knew, in the sense of having them on his calling list—and being on theirs. . . . He saw the "common people" lying like a dark sea round the raft of the privileged. They excited his piqued wonder, his ardent curiosity, he built the most elaborate theories all over and round them, he observed enough of them to be able to give characteristics, phrases, and turns of mind to the retainers of the Privileged, but he never could be brought to think that he knew enough about them to let him project their lives on to paper. He noted admirably the very phraseology of Mrs. Wicks, the faithful attendant of Maisie who lived for ever in fear of being "spoken to," and with equal admirableness the point of view of poor Brooksmith, the gentleman's valet who "never *had* got his spirits up" after the loss of his one wonderful master. But if, as happens to us to-day, he had been confronted by a Radical Left clamouring that he must write about the proletariat or be lost, he would just for ever have dismissed his faithful amanuensis and relapsed into mournful silence.

He had that conscientiousness—or if you will, that precautiousness ... and that sense of duty to his public. He set himself up— and the claim was no little one—as directing his reader as to the fine shades of the psychology of a decorative and utterly refined world where it was always five o'clock. He makes the claim with the utmost equanimity again and again in his Prefaces, only abandoning it to say that if the world did not in fact contain any creatures of such hypersensibility and sensitiveness as those he rendered in his later work, the world ought, if it was to lay claim to being civilized, to contain nobody else. ... Yet he actually knew so many details of the lives of the poorer people about him in Rye that, as I have elsewhere related, I once asked him why he did not for once try his hand at something with at least the local peasantry for a *milieu*. The question was prompted more by wonder at the amazing amount he did know than by any idea that he would possibly consider having a try at it. After all, in masterpieces like *The Spoils of Poynton*, which remains for me the technical high-water mark of all James's work—and can't I remember the rapturous and shouting enthusiasm of Conrad over that story when we first read it together so that that must have been the high-water mark of Conrad's enthusiasm for the work of any other writer? In masterpieces, then, like *The Spoils of Poynton,* James, who fifteen years or so before must have been utterly foreign to the *milieu,* had got completely and mercilessly under the skin of the English ruling classes. So that if he could penetrate one foreignness, why not another? And I cited his other great and impeccable masterpiece, *The Real Thing,* which shows members of the ruling classes reduced by financial disaster to complete pennilessness. He replied, pausing for a moment whilst the heights of Iden with its white, thatched farmhouses formed a background to his male and vigorous personality—for it was always on the Winchelsea Road that we conversed . . . he replied then:

"My dear H, you confuse the analogies. You might say that I came to this country *from* comfortable circumstances *into* comfortably circumstanced circles. Though no further uptown than Washington Square, the Washington Square of my youth was almost infinitely divided, by gulfs, chasms, canyons, from the downtownnesses round Trinity Spire where, you understand, they worked—mysteriously and at occupations as to which we of Washington Square hadn't the very ghost of an inkling. . . . And if, as you have heard me say, the comfortably circumstanced of that day were not by any manner of means luxuriously—or even hardly so much as comfortably caparisoned or upholstered or garnished at table or horse-furnitured when they rode in their buggies . . . or, if in the Mecca of good society, internationally of the highest cultivation and nationally of all that the nation had of the illustrious to offer . . . if, then, on descending the steps of the Capitol *on trébuchait sur des vaches* as the Marquis de Sabran-Penthièvre remarked in the seventies . . . if they still, at Washington, D. C., not Square, they still, to the embarrassment of the feet of visiting diplomatists, pastured cows on the lawns outside the White House, nevertheless the frame of mind . . . the frame of mind, and that's the important thing, was equally, for the supporters of the initials as for those of the Square, that of all the most comfortable that the world had to offer. . . . I do not suppose that, with the exception of the just-landed relatives of my parents' Nancies or Biddies or Bridgets in the kitchen visiting their kinsmaids, I ever saw to speak to a single human being who did not, as the phrase is—and Heaven knows, more than the phrase is and desperate and dark and hideously insupportable the condition must be—the verb's coming now ... didn't know where their next day's meals were coming from ... who were, that is to say, of that frame of mind, that, as the lamentable song says: 'They lived in a dive and sometimes contrived to pick up a copper or two.' ... For of course, as you were kind enough to say, in *The Real Thing* I have sufficiently well rendered the perturbations of the English comfortable who by financial disaster were reduced, literally, to complete vagueness as to the provenance of their next day's breakfast, lunch, tea, and dinner.... Or, as in the sketch—it isn't sufficiently complete of the more than reduced circumstances of the fathers of Kate Croy in m ... mmm...." He stopped and surveyed me with a roguish and carefully simulated embarrassment. For it was established sufficiently between us that in the longish, leanish, fairish Englishman who was Merton Densher of *The Wings of the Dove,* he had made an at least external portrait of myself at a time when he had known me only vaguely and hadn't imagined that in the ordinary course of things the acquaintance would deepen.... So he began again:

"Consider," he said with a sort of appalled vehemence, "what it must be—how desperate and dark and abhorrent—to live in such tenebrousness that all the light that could fall into your cavern must come in through a tiny orifice which, if it were shuttered by a penny, would give you light, warmth, sustenance, society, even ... and that, if it were absent, that penny would disclose nothing but unmeasured blackness that penetrated to and pervaded your miserable lair.... All light, all hope, all chance in life or of heaven dependent from that tiny disc of metal.... Why, how could you enter into a frame of mind similar to that, and still more, if you were a writer, how could you render such circumstances and all their circumambiences and implications? ... And you ask me, who *am,* for my sins, of the same vocation as the beautiful Russian genius—who am, I permit myself to say, a renderer of human vicissitudes ... of a certain conscience, of a certain scrupulousness ... you ask *me* to mislead my devotees by the

rendering of caves as to which I know nothing and as to the penetration or the mere imagination of which I truly shudder?...
Perish the thought... I say perish, perish the damnable thought.
...." He walked on for some time in a really disturbed silence,
muttering every two or three seconds to himself—and then turned
on me almost furiously.

"You understand," he said, "the damnable thought is not that
I might be poor. If I had to be poor I should hope to support the
condition with equanimity...." And he went on to explain that
it wasn't even the idea of contemplating, of delving into the
poverty of others. What he shrank from was the temptation to
treat themes that did not come into his province—the province
that he considered the one in which he could work assuredly and
with a quiet conscience.

Once he stopped suddenly on the road and said, speaking
very fast:

"You've read my last volume?... There's a story in it...." He
continued gazing intently at me, then as suddenly he began
again: "There are subjects one thinks of treating all one's life....
And one says they are not for one. And one says one must not
treat them... all one's life. All one's life.... And then suddenly
... one does... *Voilà!*" He had been speaking with almost painful agitation. He added much more calmly: "One has yielded to
temptation. One is to that extent dishonoured. One must make
the best of it."

That story was *The Great Good Place,* appearing, I think, in
the volume called *The Soft Side.* In it he considered that he had
overstepped the bounds of what he considered proper to treat—
in the way of his sort of mysticism. There were, that is to say,
mysticisms that he considered proper to treat and others whose
depths he thought should not be probed—at any rate by his pen.
For there were whole regions of his character that he never ex-
ploited in literature, and it would be the greatest mistake to forget that the strongest note in that character was a mysticism
different altogether in character from that of the great Catholic
mystics. It resembled rather a perception of a sort of fourth

dimensional penetration of the material world by strata of the supernatural, of the world of the living by individuals from among the dead. You will get a good inkling of what I mean if you will read again *The Turn of the Screw* with the constant peepings-in of the ghosts of the groom and the governess with their sense of esoteric evil—their constant peepings-in on the haunted mortals of the story. For him, good and evil were not represented by acts; they were something present in the circumambience of the actual world, something spiritual attendant on actions or words. As such he rendered them and, once convinced that he had got that sense in, he was content—he even took an impish pleasure in leaving out the renderings of the evil actions.

Of that you can read sufficiently in his enormous and affrighting Prefaces.... He never specifies in *The Turn of the Screw* what were the evil deeds of the ghostly visitants, nor what the nature of the corruption into which the children fell. And, says he in the Preface to the story:

> Only make the reader's vision of evil intense enough, I said to myself—and that is already a charming job—and his own experience, his own sympathy (with the children) and horror (of their false friends) will supply him quite sufficiently with all the particulars. Make him *think* the evil, make him think it for himself, and you are released from weak specifications.

It is an admirable artistic maxim. But it did not—and that is what I am trying to emphasize as the main note of this paper—dispense him, in his own mind, from having all the knowledges, whether of esoteric sin or the mentality of butlers, that were necessary to make him feel that he knew enough about his subject to influence the reader's vision in the right direction. As far as I know—and if diligence in reading the works of James gives one the right to know, I ought to have that right—not a single rendering of esoteric sin, sexual incidents, or shadowing of obscenities exists in all the works of the Master, and his answer to D. H. Lawrence or to Rabelais would, for him, have been sufficiently and triumphantly expressed in the sentences I have just quoted.

But that did not prevent him—when he considered the occasion to serve—from making his conversation heroically Rabelaisian, or, for me, really horrific, on the topics of esoteric sin or sexual indulgence. I have attended at conversations between him and a queer tiny being who lay as if crumpled up on the stately sofa in James's magnificent panelled room in Lamb House—conversations that made the tall wax candles seem to me to waver in their sockets and the skin of my forehead and hands prickle with sweat. I am in these things rather squeamish; I sometimes wish I was not, but it is so and I can't help it. I don't wish to leave the impression that these conversations were carried on for purposes of lewd stimulation or irreverent ribaldry. They occurred as part of the necessary pursuit of that knowledge that permitted James to give his reader the "sense of evil." . . . And I dare say they freed him from the almost universal proneness of Anglo-Saxon writers to indulge in their works in a continually intrusive fumbling in placket-holes as Sterne called it, or in the lugubrious occupation of composing libidinous Limericks. James would utter his racy "Ho-ho-ho's" and roll his fine eyes whilst talking to his curious little friend, but they were not a whit more racy and his eyes did not roll any more than they did when he was asking a housemaid or a parson's wife for advice as to the advisability of employing a Lady's Help, or than when he was recounting urbane anecdotes at tea on his lawn to the Ladies So-and-So and So-and-So. It was all in the day's work.

Exactly what may have been his intimate conviction as to, say, what should be the proper relation of the sexes, I don't profess to know. That he demanded from the more fortunate characters in his books a certain urbanity of behaviour as long as that behaviour took place in the public eye, his books are there to prove. That either Mr. Beale Farange or Mrs. Beale committed in the circumambience of *What Maisie Knew* one or more adulteries must be obvious, since they obtained divorces in England. But the fact never came into the foreground of the book. And that he had a personal horror of letting his more august friends come into contact through him with anyone who might be even remotely suspected of marital irregularities, I know from the odd, seasonal nature of my relations with him. We met during the winters almost every day, but during the summers only by, usually telegraphed, appointment. This was because during the summer Mr. James's garden overflowed with the titled, the distinguished, the eminent in the diplomatic world . . . with all his *milieu*. And, once he had got it well fixed into his head that I was a journalist, he conceived the idea that all my friends must be illegally united with members of the opposite sex. So that it was inconceivable that my summer friends should have any chance to penetrate on to his wonderfully kept lawns. I do not think that I knew any journalists at all in those days, and I am perfectly certain that, with one very eminent exception, I did not know anyone who had been so much as a plaintiff in the shadow of the divorce courts. I was in the mood to be an English country gentleman and, for the time being, I was. . . . It happened, however, that the extraordinarily respectable wives of two eminent editors were one weekend during a certain summer staying in Winchelsea—which was a well-known tourist resort—and they took it into their heads to go and call on James at Rye.

I had hardly so much as a bowing acquaintance with them. But the next day, happening to go into Rye, I met the Old Man down by the harbour. Just at the point where we met was a coal yard whose proprietor had the same name as one of the husbands of one of those ladies. James stopped short and with a face working with fury pointed his stick at the coal man's name above the gate and brought out the exasperated words:

"A couple of jaded . . . WANTONS! . . ." and, realizing that I was fairly quick on the uptake, nothing whatever more. . . . But, as soon as the leaves fell, there he was back on my doorstep, asking innumerable advices—as to his investments, as to what would cure the parasites of a dog, as to brands of cigars, as to where to procure cordwood, as to the effects of the Corn Laws on the landed gentry of England. . . . And I would accompany him, after he had had a cup of tea, back to his Ancient Town; and next day I would go over and drink a cup of tea with him and wait whilst he finished dictating one of his sentences to his amanuensis and then he would walk back with me to Winchelsea. . . . In that way we each got a four-mile walk a day. . . .

No, I never did get any knowledge as to how he regarded

sexual irregularities. . . . I remember he one day nearly made me jump out of my skin during a one-sided discussion as to the relative merits of Flaubert and Turgenev—the beautiful Russian genius of his youth.

Turgenev was for him perfection—in person, except that his features were a little broad, in the Slav manner; in his books; in his manners; in his social relations, which were of the highest; in what was aristocratic. But Flaubert, James went on and on hating and grumbling at to the end of his days. Flaubert had, as I have elsewhere related, once been rude to the young James. That James never mentioned. But he had subsequently received James and Turgenev in his dressing-gown. . . . It was not, of course, a dressing-gown, but a working garment—a sort of long, loose coat without revers—called a *chandail*. And if a French man of letters received you in his *chandail*, he considered it a sort of showing honour, as if he had admitted you into his working intimacy. But James never forgave that—more perhaps on account of Turgenev than himself. . . . Flaubert for ever afterwards was for him the man who worked, who thought, who received, who lived —and perhaps went to heaven in his dressing-gown! . . . In consequence he was a failure. All his books except one were failures— technical and material . . . and that one, *Madame Bovary,* if it was a success in both departments . . . well, it was nothing to write home about. And Flaubert's little *salon* in the Faubourg Saint-Honoré was "rather bare and provisional," and Flaubert cared too much for "form," and, because he backed bills for a relation, died in reduced circumstances. . . .

Flaubert was in short the sort of untidy colossus whom I might, if I had the chance, receive at Winchelsea, but who would never, never have been received on the summer lawns of Lamb House at Rye.

And suddenly Mr. James exclaimed, just at the dog-leg bend in the road between the two Ancient Towns:

"But Maupassant!!!! . . ." That man apparently was, for him, the real Prince Fortunatus amongst writers. I don't mean to say that he did not appreciate the literary importance of the author of *La Maison Tellier*—who was also the author of *Ce Cochon de*

Morin and, alas, of *Le Horla,* so that whilst in 1888 James was writing of him the words I am about to quote, that poor Prince was already gravitating towards the lunatic asylum. But, writes Mr. James:

> What makes M. de Maupassant salient is two facts: the first of which is that his gifts are remarkably strong and definite and the second that he writes directly *from* them. . . . Nothing can exceed the masculine firmness, the quiet force of his style in which every phrase is a close sequence, every epithet a paying piece. Less than anyone to-day does he beat the air; more than anyone does he hit out from the shoulder. . . .

sentiments which seem—but only seem—singular in view of the later convolutions of epithet that distinguished our Master. . . .

And those considerations in his conversation Mr. James completely omitted. On the Rye Road, Maupassant was for him the really prodigious, prodigal, magnificent, magnificently rewarded Happy Prince of the Kingdom of Letters. He had yachts, villas on the Mediterranean, "affairs," mistresses, wardrobes of the most gorgeous, grooms, the entrée into the historic salons of Paris, furnishings, overflowing bank balances . . . everything that the heart of man could require even to the perfectly authentic *de* to ally him to the nobility and a public that was commensurate with the ends of the earth . . . and then, as the top stone of that edifice, Mr. James recounted that once, when Mr. James had been invited to lunch with him, Maupassant had received him, not, be assured, in a dressing-gown, but in the society of a naked lady wearing a mask. . . . And Maupassant assured the author of *The Great Good Place* that the lady was a *femme du monde*. And Mr. James believed him. . . . Fortune could go no further than *that*! . . .

Manners, morals, and the point of view have so changed since even 1906 when Mr. James must have recounted that anecdote that I am not going to dilate upon it. And you have to remember that some years after the 1888 in which he wrote the words I have quoted, Mr. James underwent an experience that completely altered his point of view, his methods, and his entire literary practice. His earlier stages, Mr. James the Second contrived entirely—or almost entirely—to obscure in a sort of cuttlefish cloud of inter-

minable phrases. Until the middle nineties nothing could have
exceeded the masculine firmness, the quiet force of his writing,
and of no one else than himself could it more justly be written
that "less than anyone did he beat the air, more than anyone did
he hit out from the shoulder."

That is amazingly the case. I have more than once proclaimed
the fact that there were two Jameses. And yet no one could be
more overwhelmed than I at re-reading in their earliest forms,
after all these years, his early masterpieces as they were written
and before he went over and elaborated their phrases. Thus to
re-read is to realize with immense force that more than anyone
else, in the matter of approach to his subjects, Maupassant rather
than Turgenev must have been the young James's master. *Daisy
Miller*; that most wonderful *nouvelle* of all, *The Four Meetings*;
The Pupil; *The Lesson of the Master*; *The Death of the Lion*,
and all the clear, crisp, mordant stories that went between, right
up to *The Real Thing* and *In The Cage*—all these stories are of
a complete directness, an economy, even of phrase, that make
James one of the great masters of the *nouvelle*, the long or merely
longish short story.

But at a given date, after a misfortune that, for the second
time, shattered his life, and convinced him that his illusions as
to the delicacies of his "good" people of a certain *milieu* were in
fact...delusions; after that he became the creature of infinite
precautions that he was when I knew him best. I had, that is to
say, a sight—two or three sights—of him in the previous stage.
Then he resembled one of those bearded elder statesmen—the
Marquis of Salisbury, Sir Charles Dilke, or the Prince who was to
become Edward VII. He was then slightly magisterial; he cross-
questioned rather than questioned you; he was obviously of the
grand monde and of the daily habit of rubbing, on equal terms,
shoulders with the great.

But about the later James, clean-shaven, like an actor, so as
to recover what he could of the aspect of youth; nervous: his face
for ever mobile; his hands for ever gesturing; there hung continually the feeling of a forced energy, as if of a man conscious of
failure and determined to conceal mortification. He had had two

great passions—the one for a cousin whom he was to have married and who died of consumption while they were both very young, and the other for a more conspicuous but less satisfactory personage who in the end at about the time when the break occurred, let him down mercilessly after a period of years. And the tenacity of his attachments was singular and unforgetting.

> *The Wings of the Dove* [he writes in his Preface of 1909 to that novel], published in 1902, represents to my memory a very old—if I shouldn't perhaps say a very young—motive. I can scarcely remember the time when the motive on which this long-drawn fiction mainly rests was not vividly present to me. The idea, reduced to its essence, is that of a young person conscious of a great capacity for life, but early stricken and doomed, condemned to die under short respite while also enamoured of the world.... She was the last fine flower—blooming alone for the fullest attestation of her freedom—of an old New York stem, the happy congruities thus preserved being matters that I may not now go into, although the fine association ... shall yet elsewhere await me....

I do not know anywhere words more touching.... And I do not think that, in spite of the later obscuration, the image of the Milly Theale of that book was ever very far away from his thoughts. I remember that when, in 1906, I told him that I was going to America, his immediate reaction was to ask me to visit his cousins, the Misses Mason at Newport, Rhode Island, and to take a certain walk along the undercliff beneath Ocean Avenue and there pay, as it were, vicarious honour to the spot where, for the last time, he had parted from his dead cousin. It was the most romantic—it was the only one that was romantic—of the many small jobs that I did for him.... And in one of the fits of apologizing that would occasionally come over him—for having physically drawn myself in the portrait of Morton Densher, who was, to be sure, no hero if he wasn't more than only very subterraneously discreditable—he once said:

"After all you've got to remember that I was to fabricate a person who could decently accompany, if only in the pages of my book, another person to whom I was—and remain, and remain, Heaven knows—let us say, most tenderly attached...." As if to say that, in fabricating such a person, his mind would not let him portray someone who was completely disagreeable.

The other attachment was completely detrimental to him. Its rupture left him the person of infinite precautions that I have here rather disproportionately limned. It was as if, from then on, he was determined that nobody or nothing—no society coterie, no tram-conductor, no housemaid, no *femme du monde*—should ever have the chance, either in life or in his books, to let him down. And it was as if he said the very same thing to the phrases that he wrote. If he was continuously parenthetic, it was in the determination that no word he wrote should ever be misinterpreted, and if he is, in his later work, bewildering, it was because of the almost panicked resolve to be dazzlingly clear. Because of that he could never let his phrases alone. . . . How often when waiting for him to go for a walk haven't I heard him say whilst dictating the finish of a phrase:

"No, no, Miss Dash . . . that is not clear. . . . Insert before 'we all are' . . . Let me see. . . . Yes, insert 'not so much locally, though to be sure we're here; but temperamentally, in a manner of speaking.' " . . . So that the phrase, blindingly clear to him by that time, when completed would run:

So that here, not so much locally, though to be sure we're here, but at least temperamentally in a manner of speaking, we all are.

No doubt the habit of dictating had something to do with these convolutions, and the truth of the matter is that during these later years he wrote far more for the ear of his amanuensis than for the eye of the eventual reader. So that, if you will try the experiment of reading him aloud and with expression, you will find his even latest pages relatively plain to understand. But, far more than that, the underlying factor in his later work was the endless determination to add more and more detail, so that the exact illusions and the exact facts of life may appear, and so that everything may be blindingly clear even to a little child. . . . For I have heard him explain with the same profusion of detail as he gave to my appalled and bewildered housemaid—I have heard him explain to Conrad's son of five why he wore a particular hat whose unusual shape had attracted the child's attention. He was determined to present to the world the real, right thing!

I will quote, to conclude, the description of myself as it appears in *The Wings of the Dove* so that you may have some idea of what was James's image of the rather silent person who walked so often beside him on the Rye Road.

He was a longish, leanish [alas, alas!], fairish young Englishman, not unamenable on certain sides to classification—as for instance being a gentleman, by being rather specifically one of the educated, one of the generally sound and generally civil; yet, though to that degree neither extraordinary nor abnormal, he would have failed to play straight into an observer's hands. He was young for the House of Commons; he was loose for the Army. He was refined, as might have been said, for the City and, quite apart from the cut of his cloth, sceptical, it might have been felt, for the Church. On the other hand he was credulous for diplomacy, or perhaps even for science, while he was perhaps at the same time too much in his real senses for poetry and yet too little in them for art.... The difficulty with Densher was that he looked vague without looking weak—idle without looking empty. It was the accident possibly of his long legs which were apt to stretch themselves; of his straight hair, and well-shaped head, never, the latter neatly smooth and apt into the bargain ... to throw itself suddenly back and, supported behind by his uplifted arms and interlocked hands, place him for unconscionable periods in communion with the ceiling, the tree-tops, the sky....

That, I suppose, was the young man that James rather liked.

Ford Madox Ford, "Henry James," *Mightier Than the Sword* (London: George Allen and Unwin, 1938), pp. 13–37. This volume appeared earlier in the United States under the title *Portraits from Life* (Boston: Houghton Mifflin Co., 1937).

Introduction to *A Farewell to Arms*

When arrangements were being made to edit The Transatlantic Review *in 1924, Ezra Pound introduced a young American writer called Ernest Hemingway to Ford and suggested that he be employed unofficially as a sub-editor. To this idea Ford acceded, and soon Hemingway was reading bundles of unsolicited manuscripts on the quayside overlooking the Seine. He was also a frequent contributor to the review, and for a short period of time, during Ford's absence, he became acting editor. Altogether, Hemingway's connection with the* Transatlantic *gave him a position in Paris which helped to further his literary career.*

In 1932, when the Modern Library reissued A Farewell to Arms, *Ford was asked, as a representative of the older literary generation, to write an introduction for the edition, as he had done for so many other books by younger writers. This introduction, like the essay on James, is a work of critical impressionism, but here Ford's admiration for Hemingway's technical achievement overshadows everything else. Hemingway's clear, sparse sentences represented the kind of prose Ford himself most admired, and his act of homage to a younger artist is proof of his genuine love of literary excellence.*

I experienced a singular sensation on reading the first sentence of *A Farewell to Arms.* There are sensations you cannot describe. You may know what causes them but you cannot tell what portions of your mind they affect nor yet, possibly, what parts of your physical entity. I can only say that it was as if I had found at last again something shining after a long delving amongst dust. I daresay prospectors after gold or diamonds feel something like that. But theirs can hardly be so coldly clear an emotion, or one so impersonal. The three impeccable writers of English prose that I have come across in fifty years or so of reading in search of English prose have been Joseph Conrad, W. H. Hudson . . . and Ernest Hemingway. . . . Impeccable each after his kind! I remember with equal clarity and equal indefinableness my sensation on first reading a sentence of each. With the Conrad it was like being overwhelmed by a great, unhastening wave. With the Hudson it was like lying on one's back and looking up into a clear, still sky. With the Hemingway it was just excitement. Like waiting at the side of a coppice, when foxhunting, for the hounds to break cover. One was going on a long chase in dry clear weather, one did not know in what direction or over what country.

The first sentence of Hemingway that I ever came across was not of course:

> In the late summer of that year we lived in a house in a village that looked across the river and the plain towards the mountains.

That is the opening of *Farewell to Arms.* No, my first sentence of Hemingway was:

"Everybody was drunk." *Tout court!* Like that!

Exactly how much my emotion gained from immediately afterwards reading the rest of the paragraph I can't say.

It runs for the next few sentences as follows:

> Everybody was drunk. The whole battery was drunk going along the road in the dark. We were going to the Champagne. The lieutenant kept riding his horse out into the fields and saying to him, "I'm drunk, I tell you, mon vieux. Oh, I am so soused." We went along the road in the dark and the adjutant kept riding up alongside my kitchen and saying, "You must put it out. It is dangerous. It will be observed."

I am reading from "*N° 3 of 170 hand-made copies printed on* rives *hand-made paper.*" which is inscribed: "to robert mcalmon and william bird *publishers of the city of paris* and to captain edward dorman-smith m.c., of *his majesty's fifth fusiliers* this book is respectfully dedicated." The title page, curiously enough bears the date 1924 but the copy is inscribed to me by Ernest Hemingway "march 1923" and must, as far as I can remember have been given to me then. There is a nice problem for bibliophiles.

This book is the first version of *In Our Time* and is described as published at "paris, *printed at* the three mountains press *and for sale at* shakespeare & company *in the rue de l'odéon; london:* william jackson, *took's court, cursitor street, chancery lane."*

Those were the brave times in Paris when William Bird and I, and I daresay Hemingway too believed, I don't know why, that salvation could be found in leaving out capitals. We printed and published in a domed wine-vault, exceedingly old and cramped, on the Ile St. Louis with a grey view on the Seine below the Quais. It must have been salvation we aspired to for thoughts of fortune seldom came near us and Fortune herself, never. Publisher Bird printed his books beautifully at a great old seventeenth-century press and we all took hands at pulling its immense levers about. I "edited" in a gallery like a bird-cage at the top of the vault. It was so low that I could never stand up. Ezra also "edited" somewhere, I daresay, in the rue Notre Dame des Champs. At any rate the last page but one of *In Our Time*—or perhaps it is the *feuille de garde,* carries the announcement:

Here ends *The Inquest* into the state of
contemporary English prose, as
edited by EZRA POUND and printed at
the THREE MOUNTAINS PRESS. The six
works constituting the series are:
Indiscretions *of* Ezra Pound
Women and Men *by* Ford Madox Ford
Elimus *by* B. C. Windeler
with Designs *by* D. Shakespear
The Great American Novel
by William Carlos Williams
England *by* B. M. G. Adams
In Our Time *by* Ernest Hemingway
with portrait *by* Henry Strater.

Mr. Pound, you perceive did believe in CAPITALS and so obviously did one half of Hemingway for his other book of the same date—a blue-grey pamphlet—announces itself all in capitals of great baldness. (They are I believe of the style called *sans-sérif*):

THREE STORIES
& TEN POEMS
ERNEST HEMINGWAY

it calls itself without even a '*by*' in italics. There is no date or publisher's or distributor's name or address on the title page but the back of the half-title bears the small notices

Copyright 1923 by the author
Published by
Contact Publishing Co.

and the last page but one has the announcement

PRINTED AT DIJON
BY
MAURICE DARANTIERE
M. CX. XXIII

This copy bears an inscription in the handwriting of Mr. Hemingway to the effect that it was given to me in Paris by himself in 924. That seems almost an exaggeration in antedating.

Anyhow, I read first *In Our Time* and then "My Old Man" in *Ten Stories* both in 1923. . . .

Those were exciting times in Paris. The Young-American literature that today forms the most important phase of the literary world anywhere was getting itself born there. And those were birth-throes!

Young America from the limitless prairies leapt, released, on Paris. They stampeded with the madness of colts when you let down the slip-rails between dried pasture and green. The noise of their advancing drowned all sounds. Their innumerable forms hid the very trees on the boulevards. Their perpetual motion made you dizzy. The falling plane-leaves that are the distinguishing mark of grey, quiet Paris, were crushed under foot and vanished like flakes of snow in tormented seas.

I might have been described as—by comparison—a nice, quiet gentleman for an elderly tea-party. And there I was between, as it were, the too quiet æstheticisms of William Bird, publisher supported by Ezra Pound, poet-editor, and, at the other extreme, Robert McAlmon, damn-your-damn-highbrow-eyes author-publisher, backed by a whole Horde of Montparnasse from anywhere between North Dakota and Missouri. . . . You should have seen those Thursday tea-parties at the uncapitalled *transatlantic review* offices! The French speak of "la semaine à deux jeudis" . . . the week with two Thursdays in it. Mine seemed to contain sixty, judging by the noise, lung-power, crashing in, and denunciation. They sat on forms—school benches—cramped round Bird's great hand press. On the top of it was an iron eagle. A seventeenth-century eagle!

Where exactly between William Bird, hand-printer and publisher and Robert McAlmon, nine-hundred horse power linotype-publisher Hemingway came in I never quite found out. He was presented to me by Ezra and Bill Bird and had rather the aspect of an Eton-Oxford, husky-ish young captain of a midland regiment of His Britannic Majesty. In that capacity he entered the phalanxes of the *transatlantic review*. I forget what his official title was. He was perhaps joint-editor—or an advisory or consulting or vetoing editor. Of those there was a considerable company. I, I have omitted to say, was supposed to be Editor in Chief. They all shouted at me: I did not know how to write, or knew too much to be able to write, or did not know how to edit, or keep accounts, or sing 'Franky & Johnny,' or order a dinner. The ceiling was vaulted, the plane-leaves drifted down on the quays outside; the grey Seine flowed softly.

Into the animated din would drift Hemingway, balancing on the point of his toes, feinting at my head with hands as large as hams and relating sinister stories of Paris landlords. He told them with singularly choice words in a slow voice. He still struck me as disciplined. Even captains of his majesty's fifth fusiliers are sometimes amateur pugilists and now and then dance on their toe-points in private. I noticed less however of Eton and Oxford. He seemed more a creature of wild adventures amongst steers in infinitudes.

All the same, when I went to New York, I confided that review to him. I gave him strict injunctions as to whom not to print and above all whom not to cut.

The last mortal enemy he made for me died yesterday. Hemingway had cut *his* article and all those of my most cherished and awful contributors down to a line or two apiece. In return he had printed all *his* wildest friends *in extenso*. So that uncapitalised review died. I don't say that it died of Hemingway. I still knew he must somehow be disciplined.

But, a day or two after my return, we were all lunching in the little bistro that was next to the office. There were a great many people and each of them was accusing me of some different incapacity. At last Hemingway extended an enormous seeming ham under my nose. He shouted. What he shouted I could not hear but I realised I had a pencil. Under the shadow of that vast and menacing object I wrote verses on the tablecloth.

> Heaven over-arches earth and sea
> Earth sadness and sea-hurricanes.
> Heaven over-arches you and me.
> A little while and we shall be
> Please God, where there is no more sea
>   And no . . .

The reader may supply the rhyme.

That was the birth of a nation.

At any rate if America counts in the comity of civilised nations it is by her new writers that she has achieved that immense feat. So it seems to me. The reader trained in other schools of thought must bear with it. A nation exists by its laws, inventions, mass-products. It lives for other nations by its arts.

I do not propose here to mention other names than those of Ernest Hemingway. It is not my business to appraise. Appraisements imply censures and it is not one writer's business to censure others. A writer should expound other writers or let them alone.

When I thought that Hemingway had discipline I was not mistaken. He had then and still has the discipline that makes you avoid temptation in the selection of words and the discipline that lets you be remorselessly economical in the number that you employ. If, as writer you have those disciplined knowledges or instincts, you may prize fight or do what you like with the rest of your time.

The curse of English prose is that English words have double effects. They have their literal meanings and then associations they attain from other writers that have used them. These associations as often as not come from the Authorised Version or the Book of Common Prayer. You use a combination of words once used by Archbishop Cranmer or Archbishop Warham or the Translators in the XVI & XVII centuries. You expect to get from them an overtone of awfulness, or erudition or romance or pomposity. So your prose dies.

Hemingway's words strike you, each one, as if they were pebbles fetched fresh from a brook. They live and shine, each in its place. So one of his pages has the effect of a brook-bottom into which you look down through the flowing water. The words form a tessellation, each in order beside the other.

It is a very great quality. It is indeed the supreme quality of the written art of the moment. It is a great part of what makes literature come into its own at such rare times as it achieves that feat. Books lose their hold on you as soon as the words in which they are written or demoded or too usual the one following the other. The aim—the achievement—of the great prose writer is to use words so that they shall seem new and alive because of their juxtaposition with other words. This gift Hemingway has supremely. Any sentence of his taken at random will hold your attention. And irresistibly. It does not matter where you take it.

I was in under the canvas with guns. They smelled cleanly of oil and grease. I lay and listened to the rain on the canvas and the clicking of the car over the rails. There was a little light came through and I lay and looked at the guns.

You could not begin that first sentence and not finish the passage.

That is a great part of this author's gift. Yet it is not only "gift." You cannot throw yourself into a frame of mind and just write and get that effect. Your mind has to choose each word and your ear has to test it until by long disciplining of mind and ear you can no longer go wrong.

That disciplining through which you must put yourself is all the more difficult in that it must be gone through in solitude. You cannot watch the man next to you in the ranks smartly manipulating his side-arms nor do you hear any word of command by which to time yourself.

On the other hand a writer holds a reader by his temperament. That is his true "gift"—what he receives from whoever sends him into the world. It arises from how you look at things. If you look at and render things so that they appear new to the reader you will hold his attention. If what you give him appears familiar or half familiar his attention will wander. Hemingway's use of the word "cleanly" is an instance of what I have just been saying. The guns smelled cleanly of oil and grease. Oil and grease are not usually associated in the mind with a clean smell. Yet at the minutest reflection you realise that the oil and grease on the clean metal of big guns are not dirt. So the adverb is just. You have had a moment of surprise and then your knowledge is added to. The word "author" means "someone who adds to your consciousness."

When, in those old days, Hemingway used to tell stories of his Paris landlords he used to be hesitant, to pause between words and then to speak gently but with great decision. His temperament was selecting the instances he should narrate, his mind selecting the words to employ. The impression was one of a person using restraint at the biddings of discipline. It was the right impression to have had.

He maintains his hold on himself up to the last word of every unit of his prose. The last words of "My Old Man" are:

But I don't know. Seems like when they get started they don't leave a guy nothing.

The last words of *In Our Time:*

It was very jolly. We talked for a long time. Like all Greeks he wanted to go to America.

A Farewell to Arms end incomparably:

But after I had got them out and shut the door and turned out the light it wasn't any good. It was like saying good-by to a statue. After a while I went out and left the hospital and walked back to the hotel in the rain.

Incomparably, because that muted passage after great emotion still holds the mind after the book is finished. The interest prolongs itself and the reader is left wishing to read more of that writer's.

After the first triumphant success of a writer a certain tremulousness besets his supporters in the public. It is the second book that is going to have a rough crossing. . . . Or the third and the fourth. So after the great artistic triumph of William Bird's edition of *In Our Times* Hemingway seemed to me to falter. He produced a couple of books that I did not much like. I was probably expected not much to like them. Let us say that they were essays towards a longer form than that of the episodic *In Our Time*. Then with *Men Without Women* he proved that he retained the essential gift. In that volume there is an episodic-narrative that moves you as you will—if you are to be moved at all—be moved by episodes of the Greek Anthology. It has the same quality of serene flawlessness.

In the last paragraph I have explained the nature of my emotion when I read a year or so ago that first sentence of *Farewell to Arms*. It was more than excitement. It was excitement plus reassurance. The sentence was exactly the right opening for a long piece of work. To read it was like looking at an athlete setting out on a difficult and prolonged effort. You say, at the first movement of the limbs: "It's all right. He's in form. . . . He'll do today what he has never quite done before." And you settle luxuriantly into your seat.

So I read on after the first sentence:

In the bed of the river there were pebbles and boulders dry and white in the sun, and the water was clear and swiftly moving and blue in the channels. Troops went by the house and down the road and the dust they raised powdered the leaves of the trees. The trunks of the trees were dusty and the leaves fell early that year and we saw the troops marching along the road and the dust rising and the leaves, stirred by the freeze falling and the soldiers marching and afterwards the road bare and white except for the leaves.

I wish I could quote more, it is such pleasure to see words like that come from one's pen. But you can read it for yourself.

A Farewell to Arms is a book important in the annals of the art of writing because it proves that Hemingway, the writer of short, perfect episodes, can keep up the pace through a volume. There have been other writers of impeccable—of matchless—prose but as a rule their sustained efforts have palled because precisely of the remarkableness of the prose itself. You can hardly read *Marius the Epicurean*. You may applaud its author, Walter Pater. But *A Farewell to Arms* is without purple patches or even verbal "felicities." Whilst you are reading it you forget to applaud its author. You do not know that you are having to do with an author. You are living.

A Farewell to Arms is a book that unites the critic to the simple. You could read it and be thrilled if you had never read a book—or if you had read and measured all the good books in the world. That is the real province of the art of writing.

Hemingway has other fields to conquer. That is no censure on *A Farewell to Arms*. It is not blaming the United States to say that she has not yet annexed Nicaragua. But whatever he does can never take away from the fresh radiance of this work. It may close with tears but it is like a spring morning.

Ford Madox Ford, "Introduction" to Ernest Hemingway, *A Farewell to Arms* (Modern Library Edition; Random House, Inc., 1932), pp. ix–xx.

IMPRESSIONISM AND POETRY

Impressionism — Some Speculations

Despite his frequent assertions that for him the writing of verse was an almost automatic process, Ford in reality approached poetry in much the same way as he approached fiction. His poetry generally dealt with more emotional subjects than his prose, but as an Impressionist he relied on prose techniques to get his effects. Thus he tried to avoid emotive language and the traditional vocabulary of verse, substituting instead concrete images and precisely descriptive phrases to heighten the emotional impact of his poems.

Although today not widely remembered as a poet, Ford in the early years of the century was an influential figure. As a close friend of Ezra Pound who, with W. B. Yeats, was transforming English verse, Ford did much through his emphasis on prose techniques to stimulate this new type of verse, especially Imagist. The essay printed below was originally published, in a slightly different form, as a preface to his own Collected Poems *of 1911, and at that time it was considered to be one of the most important critical documents to have been written on modern verse.*

With regard to the actual production of verse, to the making of its form or even the evolutions of its rhythms, who would dare be exact? But, with prose, that conscious and workable medium, it is a very different matter. One finds a subject somewhere; immediately the mind gets to work upon the "form," blocks out patches of matter, of dialogue, of description.

If the function of the subject be to grow into a short story, one will start with a short, sharp, definite sentence so as to set the pace: "Mr. Lamotte," one will write, "returned from fishing. His eyes were red, the ends of his collar pressed open, because he had hung down his head in the depth of his reflection . . ."

Or, if it is to be a long short story, we shall qualify the sharpness of the opening sentence and damp it down, as thus: "When, on a late afternoon of July, Mr. Lamotte walked up from the river with his rod in his hand . . ."

Or again, if the subject seems one for a novel, we begin: "Mr. Lamotte had resided at the Brown House for sixteen years. The property consisted of six hundred and twenty acres, of which one hundred and forty were park-land intersected by the river Torridge," and so on. We shall proceed to "get in" Mr. Lamotte and his property and his ancestry and his landscape and his society. We shall think about these things for a long time and with an absolute certainty of aim; we shall know what we want to do and, to the measure of the light vouchsafed, we shall do it.

But, with verse I just do not know: I do not know anything at all. As far as I am concerned, it just comes. I hear in my head a vague rhythm. . . . I know that I would very willingly cut off my right hand to have written the *Wallfahrt nach Kevelaer* of Heine, or *Im Moos* by Annette von Dreste. I would give almost anything to have written almost any modern German lyric, or some of the ballads of my friend Levin Schücking . . . These fellows, you know . . . they sit at their high windows in German lodgings; they lean out; it is raining steadily. Opposite them is a shop where herring salad, onions and oranges are sold. A woman with a red petticoat and a black and grey check shawl goes into the shop and buys three onions, four oranges and half a kilo of herring salad . . . And there is a poem! Hang it all—there is a poem!

But this is England—this is Campden Hill and we have a literary jargon in which we must write. We *must* write in it or every word will "swear" . . .

> *Denn nach Köln am Rheine*
> *Geht die Procession. . . .*

"For the procession is going to Cologne on the Rhine." You could not use the word *procession* in an English poem. It would not be literary. Yet when those lines are recited in Germany people weep over them. I have seen fat Frankfurt bankers weeping when the *Wallfahrt* was recited in a red plush theatre with gilt cherubs all over the place . . .

I may really say that, for a quarter of a century, I have kept before me one unflinching aim—to register my own times in terms of my own time, and still more to urge those who are better poets and better prose-writers than myself to have the same aim. I suppose I have been pretty well ignored; I find no signs of my being taken seriously. It is certain that my conviction would gain immensely as soon as another soul could be found to share it. But for a man mad about writing this is a solitary world, and writing—you cannot write about writing without using foreign words—is a *métier de chien*. . . .

It is somewhat a matter of diction. In France, upon the whole, a poet—and even a quite literary poet—can write in a language that, roughly speaking, any hatter can use. In Germany, the poet writes exactly as he speaks. And these facts do so much towards influencing the poet's mind. If we cannot use the word *procession* we are apt to be precluded from thinking about processions. Now processions (to use no other example) are very interesting and suggestive things, and things that are very much part of the gnat-dance that modern life is. Because, if a people has sufficient interest in public matters to join in huge processions it has reached a certain stage of folk-consciousness. If it will not or cannot do these things it is in yet other stages. Heine's procession was, for instance, not what we should call a procession at all. With us there are definite types: there is the king's procession at Ascot; there are processions in support of women's suffrage or against it; those in support of Welsh disestablishment or against it. But the procession of Köln was a pilgrimage . . .

Organized state functions, popular expressions of desire, are one symptom; pilgrimage another; but the poet who ignores them all three is to my thinking lost; since, in one way or another, they embrace the whole of humanity and are mysterious, hazy and tangible . . . A poet of a sardonic turn of mind will find sport in describing how, in a low pot-house, an emissary of a skilful government will bribe thirty ruffians at five shillings a head to break up and so discredit a procession in favor of votes for women; yet another poet may describe how a lady in an omnibus, with a certain turn for rhetoric, will persuade the greater number of the other passengers to promise to join the procession for the saving of a church; another will become emotionalised at the sight of the Sword of Mercy borne by a peer after the Cap of Maintenance borne by yet another . . . And believe me to be perfectly sincere when I say that a poetry whose day cannot find poets for all these things is a poetry that is lacking in some of its members.

So at least, I see it. Modern life is so extraordinary, so hazy, so tenuous, with still such definite and concrete spots in it, that I am forever on the look-out for some poet who shall render it with all its values. I do not think that there was ever, as the saying is, such a chance for a poet; I am breathless, I am agitated at the thought of having it to begin upon. And yet I am aware that I can do nothing, since with me the writing of verse is not a conscious art. It is the expression of an emotion, and I can so often not put my emotions into any verse . . .

I should say, to put a personal confession on record, that the very strongest emotion, at any rate of this class, that I have ever had was when I first went to the Shepherd's Bush Exhibition and came out on a great square of white buildings all outlined with lights. There was such a lot of light—and I think that what I hope for in Heaven is an infinite clear radiance of pure light! There were crowds and crowds of people—or no, there was, spread out beneath the lights, an infinite moving mass of black, with white faces turned up to the light, moving slowly, quickly, not moving at all, being obscured, reappearing. . . .

I know that the immediate reflection will come to almost any reader that this is nonsense or an affectation. "How," he will say, "is any emotion to be roused by the mere first night of a Shepherd's Bush exhibition? Poetry is written about love; about country lanes; about the singing of birds" . . . I think it is not—not now-a-days. We are too far from these things. What we are in, that which is all around us, is the Crowd—the Crowd blindly looking for joy or for that most pathetic of all things, the good time. I think that that is why I felt so profound an emotion on that occasion. It must have been the feeling—not the thought—of all these good, kind, nice people, this immense Crowd suddenly let loose upon a sort of Tom Tiddler's ground to pick up the glittering splinters of glass that are Romance; hesitant but certain of vistas of adventure, if no more than the adventures of their own souls; like cattle in a herd suddenly let into a very rich field and hesitant before the enamel of daisies, the long herbage, the rushes fringing the stream at the end.

I think pathos and poetry are to be found beneath those lights and in those sounds—in the larking of the anaemic girls, in the shoulders of the women in evening dress, in the idealism of a pickpocket slanting through a shadow and imagining himself a hero whose end will be wealth and permanent apartments in the Savoy Hotel. For such dreamers of dreams there are.

That indeed appears to me—and I am writing as seriously as I can—the real stuff of the poetry of our day. Love in country lanes, the song of birds, moonlight—these the poet, playing for safety, and the critic trying to find something safe to praise, will deem the sure cards of the poetic pack. They seem the safe things to sentimentalise over, and it is taken for granted that sentimentalising is the business of poetry. It is not, of course. Upon the face of it the comfrey under the hedge may seem a safer card to play, for the purposes of poetry, than the portable zinc dustbin left at dawn for the dustman to take.

But it is not really; for the business of poetry is not sentimentalism so much as the putting of certain realities in certain aspects. The comfrey under the hedge, judged by these standards, is just a plant; but the ash-bucket at dawn is a symbol of poor humanity, of its aspirations, its romance, its ageing and its death. The ashes represent the sociable fires, the god of the hearth of the slumbering dawn populations; the orange peels with their bright colors represent all that is left of a little party of the night before, when an alliance between families may have failed to be cemented or, being accomplished, may prove a disillusionment or a temporary paradise. The empty tin of infant's food stands for birth; the torn scrap of a doctor's prescription for death. Yes, even if you wish to sentimentalise, the dustbin is a much safer card to play than the comfrey plant. And, similarly, the anaemic shop-girl at the exhibition, with her bad teeth and her cheap black frock, is safer than Isolde. She is more down to the ground and much more touching.

Or, again, there are the symbols of the great fine things that remain to us. Many of us might confess to being unable to pass Buckingham Palace when the Royal Standard is flying on the flagstaff without a very recognizable emotion equivalent to the journalist's phrase, a "catching at the throat." For there are symbols of aspiration everywhere. The preposterous white *papier-mâché* fountain is a symbol, so are the preposterous gilded gates, so are the geraniums and the purplish-grey pencil of Westminster Cathedral tower that overhangs the palace. There are, upon the standard, three leopards *passant* which are ancient and suggestive things; there is the lion rampant which is pretentious, and a harp which is a silly sort of thing to have upon a flag. But it is rich spot; a patch of colour that is left to us. As the ugly marquis said of the handsome footman: *"Mon dieu, comme nous les faisons— et comme ils nous font!"*

For, *papier-mâché* and *passant* leopards and all, these symbols are what the Crowd desires, and what they stand for made the Crowd what it is. And the absurd, beloved traditions continue. The excellent father of a family in jack-boots, white breeches, sword, helmet strap, gauntlets, views the preparation of his accoutrements, and the flag that he carries before his regiment, as something as much a part of his sacred profession as, to a good butler, is the family plate. That is an odd, mysterious human thing, the stuff for poetry.

We might confess again to having had emotions at the time of the beginning of the South African war—we were, say, in the gallery at Drury Lane and the audience were all on fire. We might confess to having had emotions in the Tivoli Music Hall when, just after a low comedian had "taken off" Henry VIII, it was announced that Edward VII was dying, and the whole audience stood up and sang *God Save the King*—as a genuine hymn, that time. We may have had similar emotions at seeing the little Prince of Wales standing unsteadily on a blue foot-stool at the coronation, a young boy in his Garter robes—or at a Secret Consistory at the Vatican when the Holy Father ceremonially whispered to one Cardinal or another . . .

War-like emotions, tears at the passing of a sovereign, being touched at the sight of a young prince or a sovereignly pontifical prisoner of the Vatican—this is perhaps the merest digging out of fossils from the bed of soft clay that the Crowd is. God knows we may "just despise" democracy or the writing of Laureate's odes; but the putting of the one thing in juxtaposition with the other, that seems to me to be much more the business of the poet of today than setting down on paper what he thinks about the fate of Brangaene, not because any particular "lesson" may be learned, but because such juxtapositions suggest emotions.

For myself, I have been unable to do it; I am too old perhaps or was born too late—anything you like. But there it is—I would rather read a picture in verse of the emotions and environment of a Googe Street anarchist than recapture what songs the syrens sang. That after all was what François Villon was doing for the life of his day, and I should feel that our day was doing its duty by posterity much more surely if it were doing something of the sort.

Can it then be done? In prose of course it can. But, in poetry? Is there something about the mere framing of verse, the mere sound of it in the ear, that it must at once throw its practitioner or its devotee into an artificial frame of mind? Verse presumably quickens the perceptions of its writer as does hashish or ether. But must it necessarily quicken them to the perception only of the sentimental, the false, the hackneyed aspects of life? Must it make us, because we live in cities, babble incessantly of green fields; or because we live in the twentieth century must we deem nothing poetically good that did not take place before the year 1603?

This is not saying that one should not soak oneself with the Greek traditions; study every fragment of Sappho; delve ages long in the works of Bertran de Born; translate for years like the minnelieder of Walther von der Vogelweide; or that we should forget the bardic chants of Patric of the Seven Kingdoms ... Let us do anything in the world that will widen our perceptions. We are the heirs of all the ages. But, in the end, I feel fairly assured that the purpose of all these pleasant travails is the right appreciation of such facets of our own day as God will let us perceive.

I remember seeing in a house in Hertford an American cartoon representing a dog pursuing a cat out of the door of a particularly hideous tenement house and beneath this picture was inscribed the words: "This is life—one damn thing after another." Now I think it would be better to be able to put that sentiment into lyric verse than to remake a ballad of the sorrows of Cuchulain or to paraphrase the Book of Job. I do not mean to say that Job is not picturesque; I do not mean to say that it is not a good thing to have the Book of the Seven Sorrows of whom you will in the background of your mind or even coloring your outlook. But it is better to see Life in terms of one damn thing after another, vulgar as is the phraseology or even the attitude, than to render it in terms of withering gourds and other poetic paraphernalia. It is, in fact, better to be vulgar than affected, at any rate if you practice poetry.

II

One of my friends, a Really Serious Critic, has assured me that my poem called *To All the Dead* was not worth publishing because it is just Browning. Let me, to further this speculation, just confess that I have never read Browning and that, roughly speaking, I cannot read poetry at all. I never really have been able to. And then let me analyze this case because it is the plight of many decent, serious people, friends of mine.

As boys we—I and my friends—read Shakespeare with avidity, Virgil to the extent of getting at least two Books of the Aeneid by heart, Horace with pleasure and Ovid's Persephone Rapta with delight. We liked very much the Bacchae of Euripides—I mean that we used to sit down and take a read in these things sometimes apart from the mere exigencies of the school curriculum. A little later Herrick moved us to ecstasy and some of Donne; we liked passages of Fletcher, of Marlowe, of Webster and of Kyd. At that time we really loved the Minnesingers and fell flat in admiration before anything of Heine. The Troubadors and even the Northern French Epics we could not read—French poetry did not exist for us at all. If we read a French poem at all we had always to read it twice, once to master the artificial rhythm, once for the sense.

Between seventeen and eighteen we read Rossetti, Catullus, Theocritus, Bion, Moschus, and still Shakespeare, Herrick, Heine, Elizabethan and Jacobean lyrics, Crashaw, Herbert and Donne. Towards eighteen we tried Swinburne, Tennyson, Browning and Pope. We could not read any of them—we simply and physically couldn't sit down with them in the hand long enough to master more than a few lines. We never read any Tennyson at all except for the fragment about the Eagle; never read any Swinburne at all except for a poem or two. Browning we read sufficient to "get the hang" of *Fifine at the Fair*, the *Blot on the Scutcheon* for the lyric *There's a Woman Like a Dewdrop*, and *Meeting at Night* and *Parting at Morning*, and *Oh to be in England*. . . . So that, as things go, we may be said never to have read any Browning at all. (I do not mean to say that what I did read did not influence me so that even at this late date that influence may be found in such a poem as *To all the Dead* or *The Starling*. Influences are queer things and there is no knowing when or where they may take you. But, until the other day, I should have said that Browning was the last of the poets that I should have taken consciously as a model. The other day, however,—about a month ago—my wife insisted, sorely against my wishes, on reading to me the beginning of *The Flight of the Duchess*—as far as *And the whole is our Duke's country*. . . that most triumphant expression of feudal loyalty. And my enthusiasm knew no bounds, so that, if ever the Muse should visit me again it may well be Browningese that I shall write, for there is no passage in literature that I should more desire to have written.)

But at any rate, the attempt to read Tennyson, Swinburne and Browning and Pope—in our teens—gave me and the friends I have mentioned a settled dislike for poetry that we have never since quite got over. We seemed to get from them the idea that all poets must of necessity write affectedly, at great length, with many superfluous words—that poetry, of necessity, was something boring and pretentious. And I fancy that it is because the greater part of humanity got that impression from those poets that few modern men or women read verse at all.

To such an extent did that feeling overmaster us that, although we subsequently discovered for ourselves Christina Ros-setti—who strikes us still as far and away the greatest master of words and moods that any art has produced—I am conscious that we regarded her as being far more a prose writer than a poet at all. Poetry being something pretentious, "tol-lol" as the phrase then was, portentous, brow-beating, affected—this still, small, private voice gave the impression of not being verse at all. Such a phrase describing lizards amongst heath as; *like darted lightnings here and there perceived yet nowhere dwelt upon* or such a sentence as *Quoth one, to-morrow shall be like to-day, but much more sweet*—these things gave an exquisite pleasure, but it was a pleasure comparable rather to that to be had from reading Flaubert. It was comparable rather to that which came from reading the last sentences of Herodias: *Et tous ayant pris la tête de Jokanaan s'en allaient vers Galillée. Comme elle était très lourde ils la portaient alternativement.* I do not presume to say exactly whence the pleasure comes except in so far as that I believe that such exact, formal and austere phrases can to certain men give a pleasure beyond any other. And it was this emotion that we received from Christina Rossetti.

But still, subconsciously, I am aware that we did not regard her as a poet.

And, from that day onwards I may say that we have read no poetry at all—at any rate we have read none unprofessionally until just the other day. The poets of the nineties—Dowson, Johnson, Davidson and the rest—struck us as just nuisances, writing in derivative language uninteresting matters that might have been interesting had they been expressed in the much more exquisite medium of prose. We got perhaps some pleasure from reading the poems, not the novels, of George Meredith, and a great deal from those of Mr. Hardy, whom we do regard as a great, queer, gloomy and splendid poet. We read also, by some odd impulse, the whole of Mr. Doughty's *Dawn in Britain,* that atrocious and wonderful epic in twelve volumes which is, we think, the longest and most queerly impressive poem in modern English. We read it with avidity; we could not tear ourselves away from it, and we wrote six reviews of it because no professional reviewers could be found to give the time for reading it. It was a queer adventure.

That, then, is the history of twenty years of reading verse, and I think I may say that, for men whose life-business is reading, we have read practically no poetry at all. And, during those twenty years we should have said with assurance that poetry was an artificial, a boring, an unnecessary thing.

But, about five years ago we began to think of founding a periodical—one is always thinking of founding periodicals. We had then to think of what place verse must take in the scheme of things. With our foreign ideas in which academic palms and precedence figure more strongly than they do in the minds of most freeborn islanders it did not take us long to arrive at the conclusion that poetry must have the very first place in that journal—not because it was a living force but just because it was dead and must be treated with deference. Moreover, if I may make a further confession, our express aim in founding the periodical in question, was to print a poem by Mr. Hardy, a poem that other periodicals had found too—let us say—outspoken for them to print. Now it would have been ridiculous to found an immense paper for the express purpose of printing one particular poem and not to have given that poem the utmost pride of place.

So we printed *A Sunday Morning Tragedy* first and the rest in a string after it. It seemed proper, French and traditional to do so.

And then, we began to worry our poor heads about poetry. We had, perforce, to read a great deal of it and much of what we read seemed to be better stuff than we had expected. We came for instance upon the poems of Mr. Yeats. Now, for ten or twenty years we had been making light of Mr. Yeats; we used to sniff irritably at *I will arise and go now,* and to be worried by *The Countess Kathleen.* Mr. Yeats appeared to be a merely "literary" poet; an annoying dilettante. I do not now know whether Mr. Yeats has changed or whether we have, but I am about in a moment to try to make an *amende honorable.*

At any rate we came upon the work of Mr. Yeats, of Mr. De la Mare, of Mr. Flint, of Mr. D. H. Lawrence, and upon suggestions of power in Mr. Pound's derivations from the Romance writers.

And gradually it has forced itself upon us that there is a new quality, a new power of impressionism, that is open to poetry and not so much open to prose. It is a quality that attracted us years ago to the poems of Mr. Hardy and of George Meredith. I know that my younger friends will start ominously at this announcement, that they will come round to my house and remonstrate seriously for many weary hours. But I must make the best of that.

For the fact is that, in Mr. Yeats as in Mr. Hardy, there are certain qualities that very singularly unite them, qualities not so much of diction or of mind but qualities that can only be expressed in pictorial terms. For when I think of Mr. Hardy's work I seem to see a cavernous darkness, a darkness filled with wood-smoke, touched here and there with the distant and brooding glow of smothered flame. When I think of Mr. Yeats' work I seem to see a grey, thin mist over a green landscape, the mist here and there being pierced by a sparkle of dew, by the light shot from a gem in a green cap. I have tried to write this as carefully as I can so as to express very precisely what is in the end a debt of sheer gratitude. I mean that really and truly that is the sort of feeling that I have—as if I had discovered two new countries—the country of the hardly illumined and cavernous darkness, the country of the thin grey mist over the green fields and as if those countries still remained for me to travel in.

It will at first sight appear that here is a contradicting of the words with which we set out—the statement that it is the duty of the poet to reflect his own day. But there is no contradiction. It is the duty of the poet to reflect his own day as it appears to him, as it has impressed itself upon him. Because I and my friends have, as the saying is, rolled our humps mostly in a landscape that is picked out with red patches of motor-bus sides it would be the merest provincialism to say that the author of *Innisfree* should not have sate in the cabins of County Galway or of Connemara or wherever it is, or that the author of the *Dynasts* should not have wandered about a country called Wessex reading works connected with Napoleon. We should not wish to limit Mr. Yeats' reading to the Daily Papers, nor indeed do we so limit our own, any more than we should wish to limit the author of that most beautiful impression, *The Listeners,* to the purlieus of Bedford Street where the publishers' officers are.

What worried and exasperated us in the poems of the late Lord Tennyson, the late Lewis Morris, the late William Morris, the late—well whom you like—is not their choice of subject, it is their imitative handling of matter, of words; it is their derivative attitude.

Reading is an excellent thing; it is also experience, and both Mr. Yeats and Mr. De la Mare have read a great deal. But it is an experience that one should go through not in order to acquire imitative faculties but in order to find—oneself. Roughly speaking, the late Victorian writers imitated Malory or the Laxdaela Saga and commented upon them; roughly speaking, again, the poets of today record their emotions at receiving the experience of the emotions of former writers.

The measure of the truth has to be found. It would be an obvious hypocrisy in men whose first unashamed action of the day is to open the daily paper for the cricket scores and whose poetic bag and baggage is as small as I have related—it would be an obvious hypocrisy in us to pretend to have passed the greater part of our existences in romantic woods. But it would be a similar hypocrisy in Mr. De la Mare, Mr. Yeats, or Mr. Hardy to attempt to render Life in the terms of the sort of Futurist picture that life is to me and my likes.

But to get a sort of truth, a sort of genuineness into your attitude towards the life that God makes you lead; to follow up your real preferences—to like, as some of us like, the hard, bitter, ironical German poets, the life of restaurants, of Crowds, of flashed impressions; to love as we may love, in our own way, the Blessed Virgin, Saint Katharine or the sardonic figure of Christina of Milan, and to render it, that is one good thing. Or again, to be genuinely Irish, with all the historic background of death, swords, flames, mists, sorrows, wakes and again mists; to love those things and the Irish sanctities and Paganisms—that is another good thing if it is truly rendered. The main thing is the genuine love and the faithful rendering of the received impression.

The actual language, the vernacular employed, is a secondary matter. I prefer personally the language of my own day, a language clear enough for certain matters, employing slang where slang is felicitous, and vulgarity where it seems to me that vulgarity is the only weapon against dullness. Mr. Doughty on the other hand—and Mr. Doughty is a great poet—uses a barbarous idiom as if he were chucking pieces of shale at you from the top of a rock. Mr. Yeats makes literal translations from the Irish; Mr. Hardy does not appear to bother his head much about words; he drags them in as he likes. Mr. De la Mare and Mr. Flint are rather literary, Mr. Pound, as often as not, is so unacquainted with English idioms as to be nearly unintelligible.

(God forbid, by the bye, that I should seem to arrogate to myself a position as a poet side by side with Mr. De la Mare, or, for the matter of that, with Mr. Pound. But in stating my preferences I am merely, quite humbly, trying to voice what I imagine will be the views or the aspirations, the preferences or the prejudices, of the poet of my day and circumstances when he shall at least appear and voice the life of dust, toil, discouragement, excitement and enervation that I and many millions lead today.)

When that poet does come, it seems to me, that his species will be much that of the gentlemen I have several times mentioned. His attitude towards life will be theirs; his circumstances only will be different. An elephant is an elephant whether he pours, at an African water-hole, mud and water over his free and scorched flanks, or whether, in the Zoological Gardens, he carries children about upon his back.

Ford Madox Hueffer, "Impressionism—Some Speculations," *Poetry*, II (August, September 1913), 177–187, 215–225. A variant of this essay appears in Ford's *Collected Poems* (New York: Oxford University Press, 1936).

Letter to Lucy Masterman

*In addition to stressing the use of prose techniques in verse,
Ford was anxious to bring about a change of emphasis in the
subjects normally thought suitable for poetry. During much of
the nineteenth century, and in the Victorian era in particular,
poets had tended to write about country life and medieval times.
This tradition had by no means died out, and a great many poems
written in the early years of the present century continued to
refer to pomegranates and thatched cottages. At the same time,
however, the more intelligent members of the reading public were
living in cities, where they were faced with the problems of urban
life. Since for these readers country life was unreal, poetry about
rural subjects was equally unreal, and therefore many were turning away from poetry altogether. As a poet, Ford was naturally
very concerned with this development which threatened the very
existence of poetry as a serious artistic endeavour. He therefore
urged his fellow poets to deal with life as it was actually led by
most moderns, and he suggested that instead of writing about
romantic country lanes, they write of subways and motor buses.*

*The letter printed below is one of Ford's fullest statements on
this matter. It was inspired by his reading of a volume of verse
written by the wife of one of his best friends, C. F. G. Masterman,
a Liberal politician who at one time had been a member of
Asquith's cabinet.*

SOUTH LODGE
23 January 1912

It is as you know so difficult to write anything but banalities
about one's friends' poems unless one takes them seriously, criti-
cises them and propagandises along the lines of one's own particular critical fads or canons. * * *

But after I had read a certain distance I became conscious of
a certain heaviness. It was not that the personality seemed any
less pleasant, but simply that the method, the wording was always

so much on the same note. To jump quickly to what I want to say —to what I am always wanting to say—the note is too refined, too remote, too literary. My dear lady, your poems in the future must not be written in that pleasant and sheltered verandah with the grey sea and the grey sky and all the chastened romance of it. That is holiday time. Your poetry should be your workaday life. That is what is the matter with all the verse of to-day; it is too much practiced in temples and too little in motor buses—LITER-ARY! LITERARY! Now that is the last thing that verse should ever be, for the moment a medium becomes literary it is remote from the life of the people, it is dulled, languishing, moribund and at last dead.

Yes, remember that when next you sit down to write. And sit down to write, metaphorically speaking, in a railway waiting room, or in a wet street, or in your kitchen (not in your nursery, that would be too idyllic) or in the lobby of the House of Commons, I was going to say, but the jobs that are perpetrated there are too artificial; But go where something real is doing and let your language be that of the more serious witnesses in Blue Books. My father once wrote of Rossetti that he set down the mind of Dante in the language of Shakespeare. That was clever of my father, but could there have been a greater condemnation of that magic Amateur . . . for what the poet ought to do is to write his own mind in the language of his day;

Forget about Piers Plowman, forget about Shakespeare, Keats, Yeats, Morris, the English Bible and remember only that you live in our terrific, untidy, indifferent empirical age, where not one simple problem is solved and not one single accepted idea from the past has any more any magic; Our Lord and his teachings are dead; and the late Smiles and his, and the late William Morris and John Ruskin and Newman and Froude—only that Newman was a very beautiful, unadjectival worker. It is for us to get at the new truths or to give new life to such of the old as will appeal *hominibus bonae voluntatis*. Only to do that we must do it in the clear pure language of our own day and with what is clear and new in our own individualities.

Letter in the possession of the owner, Mrs. C. F. G. Masterman.

Notes for a Lecture on Vers Libre

Essentially, Ford looked upon the writing of poetry as an expression of individual personality. For himself he therefore chose free verse as his medium, not because he was incapable of writing formally structured poems, but because he thought it artificial to force his own personality into moulds created by other poets. While this attitude is open to many objections and free verse itself has proved to be an extremely limiting technique, Ford's presentation of the case for vers libre *is refreshing and lively. More than that, it also demonstrates his real concern for the vitality of poetry and for its importance in contemporary society.*

The notes that follow, never previously printed, are taken directly from Ford's own manuscript of a lecture he gave in New York during the 1920's. It is somewhat fragmentary, but enough remains to give a clear idea of Ford's thesis.

I am going to begin by being autobiographical this evening because I want to begin by making the point that my views upon verse and verse-making are simply my own views and that I am not pretending to speak as the leader—or even as a humble member of a School. For there exists—or there did exist before the war a School of Vers Libristes who used to annex my poems and print them in their anthologies. This I accepted as a compliment—as indeed it was. And I continue to wish them all every good and to like their writings. But I cannot presume to interpret their methods, aims, or technique for the public; I can only explain my own methods and aims.

It took me, then, a long time to arrive at any conscious idea of what I wanted to do in verse—it took me perhaps twenty-five years—and then I found that I was trying to do exactly the same thing as I had always been trying to do in prose. I was trying to attain to quietude. And I remember the precise day and moment when I finally put into words exactly what I have always been trying to do. I was walking towards the sea, at the edge of a corn-field, beneath the sails of a mill, just behind someone that I was very fond of. I had been talking about poetry, through the village and along the lanes; in the corn we had to go in single file. The corn rustled and the millsails made a hurrying sort of sound and my companion being in front of me, so that I had to raise my voice a little and to talk a little more distinctly than I usually do—not much, but a little. And I said:

"I should like to write a poem—I should like to write all my poems—so that they would be like the quiet talking of some one walking along a path behind someone he loved very much—quiet, rather desultory talking, going on, stopping, with long pauses, as the quiet mind works.". . .

Then I knew that I had formulated all that I desired of literature and all that I desired to do in literature. You will say: "That is not such a Hell of a lot!"—and of course is not such a Hell of a lot. In the words of a poet who was writing about a robin, or rather who was trying to express the feelings of a robin:

> When other birds sing mortal loud, like swearing,
> When the wind lulls I try to get a hearing. . . .

You see I was born, suckled, weaned, and cradled amongst poets—poets who made great noises. And they terrified my young years and made adolescence a weariness to me. I had to listen to numbers of people like the Rossettis and Browning and Tennyson reading verse aloud. In ordinary life they were frequently agreeable enough persons. They would unbend. Rossetti taught me to make the most horrible face you could ever imagine—I would make it now, but you would not sleep after it. And my uncle William Michael Rossetti was a dear; and Christina was a kind saint, and my Aunt Lucy Rossetti was quite nice at times though too much given to the education of the young . . . But the moment any one of these normally nice people—Yes, even my grandfather, Ford Madox Brown who was the best man I ever knew—put on his or her poetic conjuring cap, life became a misery to the young growing boy. Awful warnings went from cellar to roof of the house; it must be hushed, just as if someone had died. One had to sit on chairs in the backgrounds with one's little feet well off the floors. The word had gone forth that a Poet was going to read poetry—Mrs Augusta, Philip Marston, Mathilde Blinde, Theo Marzials, Lucy Rossetti—anybody!—was going to read poetry. And just when I wanted to be going to the Round Pond to sail a model frigate!

And the most horrible changes came over these normally nice people. They had, all, always, on these occasions the aspects and voices, not only of awful High Priests before Drawing Room altars—but they held their heads at unnatural angles and appeared to be suffering the tortures of agonising souls. It was their voices that did that. They were doing what Tennyson calls, with admiration: "Mouthing out their hollow O's and A's."

And it went on and on—and on! A long, rolling stream, of words no-one would ever use, to endless monotonous, polysyllabic, unchanging rhythms, in which rhymes went unmeaningly by like the telegraph posts, every fifty yards, of a railway journey.

That was why I could never read poetry ... For I will hazard now the confession that I never could read poetry—not Shelley nor Keats; not Browning nor Tennyson. A lot of Herrick, yes! And nearly all Christina ... But that other terrifying stuff ... Never. I *could* not. ...

And it was not for want of patience, diligence, endurance. It was just inability, misery, boredom, dislike. ... I tried to read *Epipsychidion,* and I tried to read *Endymion.* I had shots at *Balaustion's Adventure* and the *Idylls of the King* and *Dante At Verona* ... I read *Goblin Market,* however, over and over again.

You see I hate—and I hated then—inversions of phrase. A line like *A sensitive plant in a garden grew* filled me with hot rage. If the chap wanted to say that a sensitive plant grew in a garden, why didn't he say it—or if he could not find a rhyme for garden, let him for Heaven's sake hold his peace. It seemed to me to be unskilful botching—and it was! I said then—and I say now—if a man cannot talk like an educated gentleman about things that matter in direct and simple English let him hold his tongue. It is a dreadful thing for a nation when its poets lose all hold on its people—and that is what has happened to England. And don't go away thinking that it is the nation that is wrong; it isn't. It is the poets.

It is the poets who are too unskilful, too lazy, too apt to mistake the obsolescent and sonorous for the beautiful and the interesting. Beauty of phrase is a most difficult thing to attain to; it is the most difficult thing in the world, simply because it is so easy to overreach into over-beauty—which causes boredom. The most beautiful prose in English of the present day is that of Mr. W. H. Hudson; it is as simple as the talking of a child. You can read it over and over again to discover the secret of the beauty—and you discover nothing. I remember discussing how Hudson wrote with Joseph Conrad and he said just that: "You can't discover anything of how Hudson writes. His words are just there, under your eyes; just as the good God makes the grass to grow." I will read you a passage—just any passage. * * *

Now that is poetry. And yet how simple it is—how absolutely open to any man to have written or to have thought. Only we can't write or think like that.

It isn't of course verse. . . . Let us then consider for a minute what verse is and can do. Verse is really the expression of a highly emotionalised state: it is therefore when it is at its best nearly always rhetorical. In its most natural form it is an expression of a passing emotion in the attempt to induce action in others. You will notice this, even nowadays, if you live much with simple and old people. Cottage folk in Kent and Sussex and Wiltshire, particularly when they are old and rather unlettered, will break into rhythmical speech quite frequently. I remember hearing an old woman in Kent who could not read lamenting the death of her daughter who was the mother of five little children. In her rhythms, in her repetitions of phrases, she spoke exactly like a Biblical character lamenting the loss of a child. I have frequently noticed this. Similarly with those other simple and unlettered beings, children, in moments of gaiety, unbending and abandon, they will almost invariably fake up some little rhyme, now and again, and will chant it in a sing song voice.

Verse-writing, then, is the easy art—it is the easiest of all the arts. Anyone can do it and most people do do it at one time or another of their careers. Prose, on the other hand, is vastly more difficult, since it is the means of expression for more sophisticated beings.

And so we have arrived at the inevitable phrase "means of expression." . . . All Art of course is just a means of expression. It is the way in which one human soul expresses itself to—or in the alternative—conceals itself from, other human beings. And, on the whole, the Art that has the greatest chance of the widest appeal, of the greatest permanence, and of the most intimate charm, is that which is the most sincere. You, have, in any art, to express your personality—and you may just as well chance your luck and express your personality as it is. For it is all very much a toss up.

Most poets fail, and the art of poetry has become discredited, usually, because poets will try to convey to the world the idea that they are more refined or more romantic than they really are, or that their eyes are not upon and their minds not occupied with, the world in which they live. The Pre-Raphaelite poets of the last century tried to give to the world the idea that their minds were exclusively occupied with beings like Isota da Rimini and with shadowy periods like the shadowy period in which lived Isota and the like. So the world suspects them—and warrantably—of insincerity and want of knowledge; the world therefore prefers to read the *Daily Mail*—which does not know anything but which to the measure of the light vouchsafed it, has a certain sincerity. And the world is quite right.

In prose, on the other hand, there is the constant peril of what I will call the literature of public notices. Certain public notices have to be framed in prose. You get Battalion Orders: "A Coy will parade at 100hrs tomorrow the 21/3/19 for inspection by the G. O. C. Dress: Marching Order. S B R's will be carried." You get announcements in Railway carriages: "At night time when the blinds are drawn; i.e. during the period between sunset and sunrise; passengers upon alighting are particularly requested to ascertain the existence of a platform."

But of course all official prose is not necessarily execrable or imbecile. There is no reason why it should be. Stendhal, for instance, formed his style—which was a style very much after the modern heart—by the study of the Code Napoleon, and you might attain to a very good prose style by studying the better paragraphs of the M.M.L. For the attempt of the official prose writer is to say what he has to say and have done with it. He does not bother about what the reader will think of him. (It is just as well sometimes.)

And that brings us to Vers Libre. You will find in all life; you will find in all your thoughts; in all careers and all human vicissitudes one certain thing—rhythm. The rhythm of your thoughts will seem to change from day to day, upon occasions, for periods. But it won't change much. You will always think in words and sentences averaging out at about the same number of syllables. You will think only in long and involved sentences, or in short sentences alone—or in one or two or three long sentences brought up sharply by a sentence of only three or four words. But however you do phrase your thoughts to yourself, the rhythm of your thought phrases will be your personality. It will be your literary personality . . . your true one.

I don't mean to say that it will be the one you use when you write; unfortunately that is not the case. For most of us can think fairly lucidly to the measure of our personalities. A few of us can even talk lucidly, sincerely and charmingly. But over everyone of us, as soon as we get a pen in our hands, there descends a cloud—of imbecility, of pomposity. We start in to imitate somebody. Sixty per cent of us imitate the late Dr. Johnson at his worst; others imitate Stevenson; Henry James; Meredith—anybody for the moment esteemed Highbrow. And almost every Englishman, Scotchman, American or Australian, if he thinks it necessary to appear emotional or impressive will at once and automatically begin to imitate the rhythm and adopt the verbiage of the English Bible or the Prayer Book Version of the psalms.

Yet no-one thinks in those rhythms or languages. Every-one has his own rhythm—which I repeat is his personality. . . . Yes, every one has his own rhythm which is his own personality. And

every one should be content with that. There is a very beautiful
sonnet by Wordsworth beginning, "If Thou indeed derive Thy
light from Heaven," and ending "Then to the measure of the
light vouchsafed,/Shine, Poet! in thy place, and be content."
Well, the message of myself to the world, speaking as a vers-
libriste is simply that:

Shine poet in thy place and be content.

That is really what vers libre is. It is an attempt to let personalities express themselves more genuinely than they have lately
done. For the worst of verse forms is that they lead almost inevitably to imitation and almost inevitably to insincerity—and still
more inevitably to the introduction of extraneous matter. You
cannot get away from that. If you write a decasyllabic, rhymed,
eight-lined verse a certain percentage of it *must* be fake. If you
are a very great poet only a small percentage of it will be—but
still there will be a small percentage. You will write *doth love*
instead of *loves* so as to fill up the line; you will look about for a
rhyme to the word *stream* and you will find *cream* and be led
away into imaging your lady as a milkmaid—that sort of thing.
. . . And a whole breed of critics, hangers on and stableboys in
the shape of German-inspired professors of literature and philology will rise up to analyse the number of times you wrote *doth
love* instead of *loves, until* instead of *till,* and innumerable pam-
phlets will be written by other grubbers on the influence of the
pastoral poetry of Tibullus in modern English verse. So literature
is obscured. . . . The only verse-canon, then, of vers libre is to
have no other verse canon than that the phrases, the cadences and
the paragraphs shall satisfy the intimate ear of the writer himself.
Listen to this:

*[At this point Ford read selections from F. S. Flint, Ezra
Pound, and H.D. Between his readings, he commented on the intimacy and quietude of the poems and observed that they were
essentially rhythmical and that "no hollow mouthings are necessary" in reading them.]*

I don't know—but I believe I am expected to read something of my own. Now I am not really a writer of unrhymed vers libre like Mr. Flint or Mrs. Aldington or Mr. Pound. I come I suppose of an older generation; no doubt I have a different temperament —and I write usually rather longer poems. So that most of my verse if it is free enough in rhythm I reinforce with rhyme. I made the discovery that rhyme helps speed. . . .

[*Here Ford read from his own poems. The remainder of the lecture was not written out in full. Ford simply jotted down some notes upon which he extemporised. These notes follow.*]

Vers libre cameo like. More emotional than prose: more for the expression of fugitive moods: but less *rhetorical* than regular rhymed verse. Regular rhymed verse was probably doomed when printing came in and poems were no longer recited or read aloud. You can listen to it with pleasure but it looks always a little nonsensical on the printed page.

Objections to vers libre. . . . None. More forms in the world the better.

Ford Madox Ford, "Notes for a Lecture on *Vers Libre*." Typescript in the possession of Herbert Weinstock, Esq.

A SUMMARY STATEMENT

The March of Literature

The March of Literature from Confucius to Modern Times, *to give it its full title, was the last and longest book Ford ever wrote. Appropriately completed, in view of his great love for France, on 14 July 1938, it is Ford's literary testimonial, the outgrowth of all his reading and writing and the fullest statement of his literary credo. Its purpose was that easily stated but immensely difficult task of increasing an appreciation of good literature among the general public. Years of experience had shown Ford that those most likely to succeed in this assignment were not professors of literature but imaginative artists—poets, novelists, and dramatists. "For it is your hot love of your art," he wrote, "not your dry delvings in the dry bones of ana and philologies that will enable you to convey to others your strong passion." Thus this book reads like a novel—an immense saga of world writings. Not in the least academic in tone, it is a personal and idiosyncratic tour of world literature from ancient to modern times. It represents Ford working at his best as a humane man of letters.*

Because Ford employed the techniques of fiction to enliven this presentation of his critical views, it is as difficult to extract a portion from the March of Literature *as it is to reprint a chapter from one of his novels—so much of what is said being dependent on what has gone before. Therefore only two very brief extracts are given here: one summarizes Ford's central critical position while the other illustrates his view of the function of literature.*

It should be remembered that in so far as this writer and the reader are united in taste we do what the French call *faire école.* We stand for Homer and the Greek lyricists as against Virgil and the Augustan Romans; for the middle ages as against the renaissance; for the seventeenth as against the eighteenth century; for the realists as against the romantics; and, above all, for the conscious literary artist as against the inspired person who, having looked upon the wine when it was red, sets vine leaves in his hair and, seizing a pen, upon paper royal inscribes such stuff as it pleases—or perhaps does not please—God to send him.

That is, perhaps, as much as to say that we stand for the Mediterranean as against the Nordic tradition. Nearly all Mediterranean writers and critics acknowledge that if you want to write you should have some—nay, as much as possible—knowledge of the technique of your art. Nearly all Nordic writers and critics contemn the idea. * * *

And, when one says that it is necessary to read such-and-such works, that does not mean that if one has not read them one will not be able to shine—or even to keep one's place—in bookishly cultured society. It means something more subtle and personal. Thus, certain qualities are necessary to the ingredients of one's ego if one is to go through a world of unforeseen accidents with dignity and composure. It is obvious that one will hardly be a proper man unless one is acquainted with the frame of mind of, say, the Old Testament, or, let us add, Plutarch's *Lives* or the *Morte d'Arthur*. You will say that the majority of the world have not read those last two books—to which the reply is that the world is none so satisfactory a place. . . . In any case, if you have not read the Old Testament you will be out of touch with the majority of your fellow beings; if you have not read Plutarch you will not have made acquaintance with a sort of high courage and sense of responsibility expressed as it is nowhere else expressed, and if you have not read the *Morte d'Arthur* you will not know the quintessence of reckless adventure and the rarenesses of chivalry. You will not merely be a different man after you have read for the first time the letter of Sir Gawain to Sir Launcelot:

I send thee greeting and let thee have knowledge, thou flower of all noble knights that ever I saw or heard of by my day, that this day I was smitten on the old wound that thou gavest me afore the city of Berwick and through the same wound that thou gavest me I am come to my own death day, wherefore I beseech thee, Sir Launcelot, to return again unto this realm, and see my tomb and say some prayer more or less for my soul.

—but you will become acquainted with a fineness of approach between man and man that has vanished from our world—aided by Cervantes! . . . And you may be given the idea of restoring a little of that feeling, by your own conduct, to this world and if you are able to you will be the happier man. . . . And if a great— an enormous—many should read those words a great many of the ills that affect us would melt away. That is what literature is for.

Ford Madox Ford, *The March of Literature from Confucius to Modern Times* (London: George Allen and Unwin, Ltd., 1947; Second impression, 1947), pp. 486, 637–638.

Acknowledgments

Grateful acknowledgment is hereby given to Miss Janice Biala for permission to include the following materials, never previously printed, from the writings of Ford Madox Ford: A 1912 letter to Mrs. C. F. G. Masterman; selections from letters to Anthony Bertram, Esq.; "Notes for a Lecture on Vers Libre." I also wish to thank the recipients of the Ford letters included in this volume for their kindness in allowing me to use them, and the H. G. Wells Estate and the University of Illinois Library for permission to publish portions of a letter from Ford to Wells. Grateful thanks are also due Dame Rebecca West for permission to quote a portion of her letter to me, and to Herbert Weinstock, Esq., the owner of the "Vers Libre" manuscript, who was most helpful and co-operative in allowing me to make a transcript.

F. M.

Lightning Source UK Ltd.
Milton Keynes UK
UKOW01f0945150916

283042UK00001B/3/P